INDEX

ABOUT THIS BOOK..3

THE NON-CALCULATOR PAPER.......................................4

ALGEBRA...5
    Sequences and Series...5
    Sequences and Series – Applications......................................7
    Exponents and Logarithms 8
    Permutations and Combinations 11
    Binomial Expansion 12
    Proof by Induction...13
    Complex Numbers 15
    The Complex Plane 16
    De Moivre's Theorem..18

FUNCTIONS AND EQUATIONS...20
    Basics of Functions...20
    Graphs of Functions..23
    Reciprocal Functions 27
    Quadratic Functions..28
    Solving Quadratic Equations...29
    Inequalities 30
    Polynomial Functions..32
    Exponential and Logarithmic Functions..................................34

CIRCULAR FUNCTIONS AND TRIGONOMETRY 35
    Definitions and Formulae 35
    Trigonometric Formulae..38
    Solving Trigonometric Equations 39
    The Solution of Triangles 41
    Graphing Periodic Functions 42

MATRICES 43
    Basics of Matrices...43
    Determinants and Inverse Matrices..44
    Solving Equations Using Matrices...45

VECTORS...48
    Basics of Vectors..48
    Scalar (Dot) Product 50
    Vector (Cross) Product 51
    Equations of Lines 52
    Equations of Planes 53
    Equations of Lines and Planes – Summary............................54
    Intersections 55
    Angles in Three Dimensions 57
    Miscellaneous Vector Questions...58

STATISTICS AND PROBABILITY...59
    Basics of Statistics..59
    Cumulative Frequency...62
    Probability Notation and Formulae..64
    Lists and Tables of Outcomes...65
    Venn Diagrams 66
    Tree Diagrams 67
    Discrete Probability Distributions 68
    Binomial Distribution 69
    Poisson Distribution 71
    Continuous Distributions 72
    The Normal Distribution 74

CALCULUS 77
    Differentiation – The Basics 77
    Differentiation from First Principles 78

The Chain Rule 79
Product and Quotient Rules 80
Second Derivative 81
Graphical behaviour of functions 82
Sketching Graphs – Examples 83
Applications of Differentiation 84
Implicit Differentiation 86
Indefinite Integration 87
Definite Integration 89
Integration By Substitution 90
Integration by Parts 91
General Methods for Integration 92
Integration Practice 93
Differential Equations 94
Volumes of Revolution 96
Calculus – Non-Calculator Techniques 97
MAXIMISING YOUR MARKS 99
ASSESSMENT DETAILS..100
PRACTICE QUESTIONS 101
Answers to Practice Questions 106

ABOUT THIS BOOK

This is a revision book, not a text book. It will show you everything you need to know in the Math Higher syllabus, but it assumes that you have already covered the work, and that you are now going through it for the second (or third, or fourth ....) time. I would expect you to use your other resources (text book, class notes) to fill in much of the detail.

The exam is not so much a test of your knowledge and understanding (you will not get a question which begins "What do you know about ....?"); but a test of how you use your understanding to solve mathematical problems. So the emphasis in this revision book is on how to answer questions. In particular you will find plenty of worked exam style questions, as well as further ones for *you* to solve. All the questions in boxes are of a standard and of a type that could occur in your exams. Do not skim over these – much useful revision material is contained in the working which is not contained in the text.

The option topics are all quite substantial. So, rather than increase the size (and cost) of this book by including all of them here, each option topic has its own revision guide.

You are expected to be able to understand and use your graphic display calculator (GDC) in all relevant areas of the syllabus. Indeed, some questions *require* you to use, for example, the graphing or the equation solving features. Since different people use different calculators, it is not possible for this book to explain the detail of their use; but I have indicated (using the calculator symbol ▦) where the GDC can be particularly useful. If you have a calculator from the TI family, you might like to know that another book in the OSC Revision Guide series, "Using the TI calculator in IB Maths", will guide you through all the techniques you need.

This is *your* revision book. Every page has a wide column for you to make notes and scribblings and write down questions to ask your teacher; the "You Solve" questions generally have enough space for you to write down your own working. And towards the end there are some important points about how to maximise your exam mark. *Do* follow the suggestions there, and perhaps add some more of your own.

At the very end there are some practice questions testing you on the basic work contained in each area of the syllabus.

Through Oxford Study Courses I have been privileged to help many students revise towards their IB Mathematics exams, and much of what I have learnt from teaching them has been distilled into this book. I would value any feedback so that later editions can continue to help students around the world. Please feel free to e-mail me on inlucas@greentrees.fsnet.co.uk. All correspondence will be answered personally.

Ian Lucas

THE NON-CALCULATOR PAPER

Exams from 2008 onwards cover exactly the same syllabus as before, but Paper 1 is a non-calculator paper. In addition, both Papers 1 and 2 have a different format from pre-2008 exams: they both have a section A consisting of short answer questions, and a section B consisting of extended answer questions. Full details are on page 100.

It is not intended that Paper 1 will test your ability to perform complicated calculations with the potential for careless errors. It is more to see if you can analyse problems and provide reasoned solutions without using your calculator as a prop. However, this doesn't mean that there are no arithmetic calculations. You should, for example, be able to:

Add and subtract using decimals and fractions:
Examples:
$18.43 + 12.87$, $2\frac{1}{2} + 3\frac{2}{5}$

Multiply using decimals and fractions (brush up your multiplication tables):
Examples:

432×14, 12.6×5, $\frac{1}{2} \times \frac{2}{5} + \frac{2}{3} \times \frac{1}{4}$, $(2 \times 10^6) \times (5.1 \times 10^{-4})$, $\begin{pmatrix} 0.5 & 0.1 \\ -0.1 & 0.2 \end{pmatrix}\begin{pmatrix} 2 & 0.5 \\ 1 & -2 \end{pmatrix}$

Carry out simple divisions using decimals and fractions
Examples:
$14 \div 0.02$, $1\frac{1}{2} \div \frac{3}{5}$, find x as a fraction is simplest form if $999x = 324$

And don't forget that divisions can be written as fractions, eg:
$9 \div 15 = \frac{9}{15} = \frac{3}{5} = 0.6$

Fraction simplification can help with more complex calculations:

Convert 81km/h to m/s
$$\frac{81 \times 1000}{3600} = \frac{81 \times 10}{36} = \frac{9 \times 10}{4} = \frac{9 \times 5}{2} = \frac{45}{2} = 22.5\text{m/s}$$

Percentage calculations:
Examples:
15% of 600kg, Increase 2500 by 12%, what is 150 as a percentage of 500.

Quadratic equations
You will be called on to solve quadratic equations many times in the papers. Solving by factorisation is easier than using the formula when you are not using a calculator.
Examples:
Solve $x^2 + 7x - 60 = 0$; $3x^2 - 19x + 20 = 0$

NOTE: The Revision Guide contains many boxed questions which are either worked examples or practice questions. Any which would be hard to solve without a calculator will be shown with a double line (as in this box). For the remaining questions, calculator use is either irrelevant (for example, differentiating a function), or the question could be answered both with and without a calculator. In the latter case, it would be sensible for you to answer the question *without* a calculator, and then check your answer *with* a calculator.

ALGEBRA

Sequences and Series

There are many different types of number sequence. You only need to know about two: the *arithmetic sequence* (AP) and the *geometric sequence* (GP). In an AP each number is the previous number *plus* a constant. In a GP each number is the previous number *multiplied* by a constant.

A *series* is the same as a *sequence* except that the terms are added together: thus a series has a *sum*, whereas a sequence doesn't.

To answer most sequences and series questions, make sure you are familiar with the formulae below. First, the notation:

u_1 = the first term of the sequence (*many formulae use a instead*)
n = the number of terms in the sequence
l = the last term of the sequence
d = the common difference (the number added on in an AP)
r = the common ratio (the multiplier in a GP)
u_n = the value of the *n*th term
S_n = the sum of the first *n* terms
S_∞ = the sum to infinity

Examples:

Arithmetic sequences:
3, 5, 7, 9 .....
1.1, 1.3, 1.5, 1.7 .....
11, 7, 3, -1, -5 ......

Geometric Sequences:
1, 3, 9, 27 .....
4, 6, 9, 13.5 .....
12, 6, 3, 1.5, 0.75 .....
2, -6, 18, -54 ....

I use AP (Arithmetic Progression) and GP (Geometric Progression), but these are not terms used in IB.

The formulae:

For an AP:
The value of the *n*th term:
$$u_n = u_1 + (n-1)d$$
$$d = u_{n+1} - u_n$$

The sum of *n* terms:
$$S_n = \frac{n}{2}(u_1 + l) = \frac{n}{2}(2u_1 + (n-1)d)$$

For a GP:
The value of the *n*th term:
$$u_n = u_1 r^{n-1}$$
$$r = \frac{u_{n+1}}{u_n}$$

The sum of *n* terms:
$$S_n = \frac{u_1(r^n - 1)}{r-1}$$

And for GPs only there is a formula for "the sum to infinity." If the common ratio is a fraction (ie $-1 < r < 1$) then the terms get ever smaller and approach zero. In this case, the *sum* of the series will converge on a particular value. To calculate this value:

$$S_\infty = \frac{u_1}{1-r}$$

Series questions often involve algebra as well as numbers. Note that to find d given two consecutive terms in an AP, subtract the first from the second; and to find r in a GP, divide the second by the first.

The sum formulae always start from the first term. If you wanted to sum, say, the 10th to the 20th terms, you would calculate $s_{20} - s_9$. Think about it!

Sigma Notation: Sigma notation is just a shorthand for defining a series. The Σ symbol means "the sum of" and will include a general formula for the terms of the series. For example,

Example: A GP has first two terms 2 and k. What range of values of k will ensure the series converges?

The common ratio must be between −1 and 1. The common ratio is $\frac{k}{2}$, so:

$$-1 < \frac{k}{2} < 1 \text{ so } -2 < k < 2$$

$$\sum_1^4 (n^2 - 2) = (1^2 - 2) + (2^2 - 2) + (3^2 - 2) + (4^2 - 2) = 22$$

The ratio of the fourth term to the tenth term of an AP is 5:11. The sum of the first term and the third term is 18. Find the sum of the first 50 terms.

To find the sum we need a and d. This means simultaneous equations, and the information in the first two sentences should resolve into two equations.

$u_4 = a + 3d$, $u_{10} = a + 9d$. Thus, $11(a + 3d) = 5(a + 9d)$ giving $6a = 12d$ or $a = 2d$.
Also, $a + (a + 2d) = 18$, giving $a + d = 9$.

Solving these simultaneously, we get $a = 6$ and $d = 3$.

$$S_n = \frac{n}{2}(2a + (n-1)d), \quad S_{50} = \frac{50}{2}(2 \times 6 + 49 \times 3) = \underline{\textbf{3975}}$$

YOU SOLVE

The second term of a geometric sequence is 12 and the sum to infinity of the corresponding series is 50. Find the first term and the common ratio, which is greater than 0.5.

$\underline{a = 20,} \qquad \underline{r = 0.6}$

Recurring decimals: All recurring decimals are rational numbers and can therefore be written exactly as fractions. The following method can be used to find the equivalent fraction:

- Put $r =$ the decimal
- Multiply both sides by an appropriate power of 10 so that the pattern on the right hand side of the decimal point matches the original
- Subtract the two equations, then divide to find r

eg: Write 2.363636… as a fraction

$r \quad = 2.363636…$
$100r = 236.363636…$ (Now subtract)
$99r = 234 \Rightarrow r = \dfrac{234}{99}$

Sometimes it is necessary to multiply twice to get the right hand sides matching:

Express the recurring decimal 0.34253253253… as a rational number.

$r \qquad = 0.34253253253…$
$100r \quad = 34.253253253…$
$100000r = 34253.253253253…$

Subtracting, $99900r = 34219$

So $r = \dfrac{34219}{99900}$ *(although on a non-calculator paper it wouldn't be clear if this fraction simplified)*

Sequences and Series – Applications

Questions do not necessarily make it obvious that the sequence and series formulae are to be used. For example, if a ball is dropped then rises to 2m on its first bounce and then to 0.6 of its height on each subsequent bounce, then the height of each bounce is a geometric sequence with $r = 0.6$. Be careful of the difference between: "How high does it rise after 4 bounces?" and "What is the total distance travelled when it hits the ground for the 4th time?"

> The answers are 0.2592m and 6.704m

One important application of sequences and series is their use in solving financial problems involving *interest*. If a sum of money is invested, the rate of interest is the amount (expressed as a %) that it earns during each period (usually, but not necessarily, a year).

Simple interest: The interest earned is not added to the total amount which thus stays constant.

- $1000 at 5% simple interest per year will earn $50/year. In 10 years, the investment is worth $1000 + 10 \times 50 = \$1500$.

Compound interest: The interest earned is *added* to the amount invested. Thus the investment grows by a larger amount each year.

- $1000 at 5% compound interest will multiply by 1.05 each year (A 5% increase can be calculated using a multiplier of 1.05).

After 1 year, the investment is worth $1000 \times 1.05 = \$1050$
After 2 years, the investment is worth $1000 \times 1.05^2 = \$1102.50$
After n years, the investment is worth 1000×1.05^n

Note that with the simple interest, the value of the investment is increased by $50/year and will form an AP. With the compound interest, the value will increase by a factor of 1.05 each year and will form a GP.

> Beware of questions where extra money is added to the investment each year *as well as* the interest.

John invests $1000 at 6% interest, compounded annually, for 16 years.

a)   How much is the investment worth after 16 years?

b)   If John removes one quarter of the amount after 4 years, and leaves the remainder to accumulate at 6% until the end of the 16th year, find the final value.

c)   Show if John removes one quarter of the amount at *any* time, and leaves the rest to accumulate at 6%, he will always end up with the same amount as in (b).

In part (c) use n to generalise the year he takes the money out. The total amount should work out to $750 \times 1.06^n \times 1.06^{(16-n)}$. Now simplify this expression – it should not depend on n.

YOU SOLVE

$2540.35, $1905.26

Exponents and Logarithms

Exponents: Exponent is another word for power or index. You must understand the meaning of negative and fractional powers as well as positive, whole number powers. You must also be very familiar with the rules for using powers.

Let's look at powers of 2:

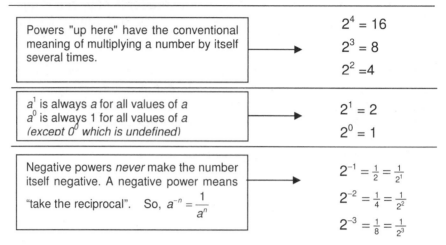

Powers "up here" have the conventional meaning of multiplying a number by itself several times.	$2^4 = 16$ $2^3 = 8$ $2^2 = 4$
a^1 is always a for all values of a a^0 is always 1 for all values of a *(except 0^0 which is undefined)*	$2^1 = 2$ $2^0 = 1$
Negative powers *never* make the number itself negative. A negative power means "take the reciprocal". So, $a^{-n} = \dfrac{1}{a^n}$	$2^{-1} = \frac{1}{2} = \frac{1}{2^1}$ $2^{-2} = \frac{1}{4} = \frac{1}{2^2}$ $2^{-3} = \frac{1}{8} = \frac{1}{2^3}$

Examples:

$2.5^1 = 2.5$

$4^{-2} = \dfrac{1}{16}$

$\left(\dfrac{2}{3}\right)^{-3} = \left(\dfrac{3^3}{2^3}\right) = \dfrac{27}{8}$

$8^{\frac{5}{3}} = \left(\sqrt[3]{8}\right)^5 = 32$

Fractional powers always involve *roots*. The power $\frac{1}{2}$ means the square root, the power $\frac{1}{3}$ means the cube root; the power $\frac{3}{2}$ means the cube of the square root. These can be combined with a negative sign to give, for example:

$$3^{-\frac{2}{5}} = \frac{1}{(\sqrt[5]{3})^2}$$

In general, $a^{\frac{1}{n}} = \sqrt[n]{a}$ and $a^{\frac{m}{n}} = \left(\sqrt[n]{a}\right)^m = \sqrt[n]{a^m}$

Laws of exponents: The rules which follow occur in all sorts of mathematical situations and you should learn them carefully:

$a^x \times a^y = a^{x+y}$ (for example, $2^{x+3} = 2^x \times 2^3 = 8 \times 2^x$)

$a^x \div a^y = a^{x-y}$ (for example, $\dfrac{x^3}{\sqrt{x}} = \dfrac{x^3}{x^{\frac{1}{2}}} = x^{3-\frac{1}{2}} = x^{\frac{5}{2}}$)

$(a^x)^y = a^{xy}$ (for example, $9^x = (3^2)^x = 3^{2x}$)

$(ab)^x = a^x b^x$ (for example, $(3x)^3 = 27x^3$)

x	$\rightarrow$	2^x
3	$\rightarrow$	8
2	$\rightarrow$	4
1	$\rightarrow$	2
0	$\rightarrow$	1
-1	$\rightarrow$	0.5
$\log_2 x$	$\leftarrow$	x

What is a logarithm? The mapping diagram on the left shows the function $f(x) = 2^x$ applied to a few integers. The inverse of this function would map $8 \rightarrow 3$, $4 \rightarrow 2$ and so on: in other words, it would find what power of 2 gives the required number. As shown at the bottom of the diagram, the inverse is the logarithm function. So the logarithm to the *base 2* of a number is the power of 2 which gives the number. For example, $\log_2 16 = 4$. It may be helpful to think of the relationship of the log(arithm) function to the power function as similar to that between the square root function and the square function.

Examples:

$$\log_3 27 = 3$$
$$\log_{10} 0.1 = -1$$
$$\log_2\left(\sqrt{2}\right) = \frac{1}{2}$$
$$\log_5\left(5^x\right) = x$$

Ensure that you are familiar with common powers of integers from 2 to 6.

$$2^2 = 4, 2^3 = 8, 2^4 = 16, 2^5 = 32, 2^6 = 64, 2^7 = 128.$$
$$3^2 = 9, 3^3 = 27, 3^4 = 81, 3^5 = 243.$$
$$4^2 = 16, 4^3 = 64, 4^4 = 256.$$
$$5^2 = 25, 5^3 = 125, 5^4 = 625.$$
$$6^2 = 36, 6^3 = 216.$$

You may literally need to know these backwards, for example to recognise that $\dfrac{1}{243} = 3^{-5}$. Such recognition would be required to solve an equation such as: $243 \times 3^{2x} = 1$

Since negative powers involve reciprocals, it is likely that questions involving negative powers will require you to manipulate fractions.

Fractional powers always involve roots. For example, $3^{\frac{2}{3}} = \sqrt[3]{3^2} = \sqrt[3]{9}$. You would need a calculator to work out this value, but the laws of exponents often allow you to simplify expressions without the use of a calculator. For example, to simplify $\dfrac{3^{\frac{1}{3}} \times 9^{\frac{2}{3}}}{\sqrt[3]{9}}$ it is necessary to recognise that 9 is an integer power of 3.

$$\frac{3^{\frac{1}{3}} \times 9^{\frac{2}{3}}}{\sqrt[3]{9}} = \frac{3^{\frac{1}{3}} \times 3^{\frac{4}{3}}}{9^{\frac{1}{3}}} = \frac{3^{\frac{5}{3}}}{3^{\frac{2}{3}}} = 3^{\frac{3}{3}} = 3$$

Surds: Make sure you are entirely familiar with the rules for manipulating surds. In particular:

$$\sqrt{a} \times \sqrt{b} = \sqrt{ab}, \quad \sqrt{a} \div \sqrt{b} = \sqrt{\frac{a}{b}}$$
$$\sqrt{a} + \sqrt{b} \neq \sqrt{a+b}, \quad \sqrt{a} - \sqrt{b} \neq \sqrt{a-b}$$

Thus:

$$\sqrt{2} \times \sqrt{18} = \sqrt{36} = 6$$
$$\sqrt{50} + \sqrt{98} = \sqrt{25}\sqrt{2} + \sqrt{49}\sqrt{2} = 5\sqrt{2} + 7\sqrt{2} = 12\sqrt{2}$$
$$\sqrt{\frac{49}{100}} = \frac{\sqrt{49}}{\sqrt{100}} = \frac{7}{10}$$

It is sometimes useful when manipulating surds to think of the rules of algebra – in the second example above, compare $5\sqrt{2} + 7\sqrt{2}$ with $5x + 7x$. This should enable you to quickly calculate the values of $(4\sqrt{3})^2$ and $(2 + \sqrt{5})(2 - \sqrt{5})$ (*Answers:* 48 and -1).

You should also be able to *rationalise* the denominators of fractions which contain surds. If the denominator is of the form $\sqrt{a}$, then multiply numerator and denominator by $\sqrt{a}$; if the denominator is of the form $a + \sqrt{b}$, then multiply numerator and denominator by $a - \sqrt{b}$. In both cases, the denominator will become a rational number. (The process is very similar to the division of complex numbers).
Example:

$$\frac{4}{3 - \sqrt{3}} = \frac{4}{3 - \sqrt{3}} \times \frac{3 + \sqrt{3}}{3 + \sqrt{3}} = \frac{12 + 4\sqrt{3}}{9 - 3} = \frac{12 + 4\sqrt{3}}{6} \text{ or } 2 + \frac{2\sqrt{3}}{3}$$

Change of base: Logarithms can be to any base, but your calculator only has two: base 10 and base e. If a logarithm is not straightforward (such as the examples above), use the change of base formula:

$$\log_a b = \frac{\log_c b}{\log_c a}$$

eg: $\log_4 12 = \frac{\log_{10} 12}{\log_{10} 4} = 1.79$ *(by calculator)*   *(Check: $4^{1.79} \approx 12$)*

Laws of logarithms: Because logarithms are just powers, the laws of logarithms are very similar to the laws of exponents. You should be very familiar with them. These rules apply to logs with any base.

- $\log a + \log b = \log(ab)$
- $\log a - \log b = \log(a/b)$
- $\log a^n = n\log a$

A common mistake is to write $\log a x^2$ as $2\log ax$. This would only work if the square applied to the a as well. But we could also use the first law to get:
$\log ax^2 = \log a + \log x^2 = \log a + 2\log x$

The last gives a useful method for solving equations with powers in because it can be used to "bring the power down."

Example: Solve $2^x = 13$

The logs can be to any base, so in practice use the log *key on your calculator (ie base 10)*

$2^x = 13$
$\log(2^x) = \log 13$
$x \log 2 = \log 13$
$x = \frac{\log 13}{\log 2} = 3.70$

$\log_{10}A = x$, $\log_{10}B = y$, $\log_{10}C = z$. **Express $\log_{10}\left(\dfrac{A}{BC^2}\right)^3$ in terms of x, y and z.**

Use the laws of logarithms one at a time to sort out the algebraic expression.

$\log_{10}\left(\dfrac{A}{BC^2}\right)^3 = 3(\log_{10} A - \log_{10} BC^2) = 3(\log_{10} A - (\log_{10} B + \log_{10} C^2)) = 3(\log_{10} A - \log_{10} B - 2\log_{10} C)$

Now substitute the x, y and z to get **$3x - 3y - 6z$**

---

e^x and $\ln x$:   Functions such as 2^x and 3^x are called "exponential functions"; e^x is called "*the* exponential function" because of its importance in modelling functions such as population growth. Like π, e is an irrational number and has an approximate value of 2.718... Its inverse is $\log_e x$ which is normally written as $\ln x$.

Note that $e^{\ln x} = x$ and $\ln e^x = x$. Use this when simplifying expressions, solving equations or changing the subject of the formula. This rule is true for logs to any base.

If $p = 3 + 2e^{0.04t}$, find t when $p = 7.63$.

So $7.63 = 3 + 2e^{0.04t} \Rightarrow 2.315 = e^{0.04t}$
Now "ln" both sides: $\ln 2.315 = \ln e^{0.04t}$
$\ln 2.315 = 0.04t$
$\dfrac{\ln 2.315}{0.04} = t$ so $t = 21.0$

Permutations and Combinations

Use *combinations* when you want to select a certain number of objects from a group, but order is unimportant. Use *permutations* when you want to both select and arrange the objects.

The multiplication principle: If there are 2 ways of choosing an option A and 3 ways of choosing an option B, then there will be $2 \times 3 = 6$ ways of choosing option A followed by B. For example, when you throw a die then toss a coin there will be $6 \times 2 = 12$ possible outcomes.

Combinations: The combinatorial formula $^nC_r = \dfrac{n!}{r!(n-r)!}$

> Sometimes written as $\dbinom{n}{r}$

will calculate the number of ways of selecting r objects from n. When using this formula without a calculator, it is not necessary to know the factorials of large numbers – use simplification of fractions. For example,

$$^7C_3 = \frac{7!}{3!4!} = \frac{7 \times 6 \times 5}{3 \times 2 \times 1} = \frac{7 \times 5}{1} = 35$$

Note how the 4! In the denominator cancels with the tail of the 7!, and then the 3×2 cancels with the 6. It is also useful to remember that $^nC_0 = {}^nC_n = 1$, and $^nC_1 = n$.

Thus, if you have to choose a committee of 4 from 13 people, the number of possible choices is $^{13}C_4 = 715$. What if the 13 consists of 8 men and 5 women, and you want to choose 2 of each? Using the multiplication principle this becomes $^8C_2 \times {}^5C_2 = 280$.

> We could also turn this into a probability: eg: *You are choosing a committee of 4 from 13 people. What is the probability that the committee will consist of 2 men and 2 women?*
>
> Answer: $\frac{280}{715} = 0.392$

Sometimes constraints are put in. For example:

A football team (11 people) is to be chosen from 15. The captain must be selected, as must one of the two possible goalkeepers. How many possible teams could be chosen?
In effect, we must select 1 from 1, 1 from 2 and then 9 from the remaining 12. So the calculation is $^1C_1 \times {}^2C_1 \times {}^{12}C_9 = 440$.

Permutations: First, remember that there are $n!$ ways of arranging n objects. When *selecting* some objects before arranging them, I use the "boxes" method. For example, in how many ways can you choose a first and a second prize winner from 6 dogs in a dog show?

	Draw two boxes		
6 possibilities for the first box		6	
5 possibilities for the second box		6	5

Thus there are 30 possible arrangements.

---

a) Find the number of integers that can be formed using the digits 1,2,3,4 if each digit can only be used once.

<u>24</u>

b) With the same four digits, find how many integers between 1000 and 4000 can be formed. *Draw four boxes. How many possibilities are there for the first box? Then carry on for the other boxes.*

<u>18</u>

YOU SOLVE

Binomial Expansion

Pascal's Triangle: It is helpful to remember the first few rows of Pascal's Triangle.

You can create a complete row of Pascal's triangle by using a list instead of the value of r. Or by inputting the function $5^{n}C_{r} x$ (for the fifth row, say) and setting up a table with x from 0 to 5.

Each number can also be calculated using the combinatorial formula. For example, the 6th row, 2nd column (starting at column 0) is $^{6}C_{2} = 15$. Sometimes

$$
\begin{array}{ccccccccccccc}
 & & & & & & 1 & & 1 & & & & \\
 & & & & & 1 & & 2 & & 1 & & & \\
 & & & & 1 & & 3 & & 3 & & 1 & & \\
 & & & 1 & & 4 & & 6 & & 4 & & 1 & \\
 & & 1 & & 5 & & 10 & & 10 & & 5 & & 1 \\
 & 1 & & 6 & & 15 & & 20 & & 15 & & 6 & & 1
\end{array}
$$

the alternative notation $\binom{6}{2}$ is used, but this can be confusing because it looks like a vector!

The Binomial Expansion: The general formula gives you a quick way of multiplying out brackets of the form $(a + b)^n$ where n is a natural number. It is best illustrated with an example.

To expand $(a + b)^4$ each term will have 3 parts to it:
- The appropriate Pascal's Triangle number (in this case using row 4);
- a to a power beginning at 4 and reducing to 0;
- b to a power beginning at 0 and increasing to 4.

The 1's that result in the first and last terms reduce those terms to a^4 and b^4.

Note that the total of the powers of a and b in each term is always 4.

$$(a + b)^4 = a^4 + 4a^3b + 6a^2b^2 + 4ab^3 + b^4$$

This general form can now be used to expand more specific expressions, for example $(2 - 3x)^4$. When doing this, note:
- Always write out the general form first, then substitute underneath (in this case, $a = 2$, $b = -3x$).
- Use brackets throughout to ensure correct calculation.
- Use one line to substitute, the next to calculate.

Be careful when substituting a negative number – always use brackets.

$$(2 - 3x)^4 = 2^4 + 4(2)^3(-3x) + 6(2)^2(-3x)^2 + 4(2)(-3x)^3 + (-3x)^4$$

$$= 16 - 96x + 216x^2 - 216x^3 + 81x^4$$

Find the value of a ($a \neq 0$) if the coefficients of x^2 and x^3 in the expansion of $(2 - ax)^5$ are equal.

The powers of x in the 6 terms will be: x^0, x^1, x^2, x^3, x^4 and x^5. The corresponding Pascal's triangle numbers are 1, 5, 10, 10, 5, 1. So the terms in x^2 and x^3 are:

$10 \times 2^3 \times (-ax)^2$ and $10 \times 2^2 \times (-ax)^3$ *(In each term, the powers always add up to 5).*

Thus the *coefficients* are $80a^2$ and $-40a^3$

So, $80a^2 = -40a^3 \Rightarrow \underline{\boldsymbol{a = -2}}$

YOU SOLVE

Find the coefficient of x^5 in the expansion of $(2x - 5)^8$

-224000

Proof by Induction

Induction is used to prove a general result on the set of natural numbers which has already been obtained by surmise or guesswork. A question could begin: "Prove by induction that, for n > 0, ..." The method to follow is:

- Show the result is true for the first value of n (usually 1);
- Then show that if the result holds for some general value (say, k) then it will also hold for $k + 1$. This will require some means of moving from the kth result to the $(k + 1)$th, depending on the type of question.

The second part often involves heavy algebra: don't then forget the first part which is usually a simple substitution.

The most common proofs you are asked to carry out are:

- General formula for the sum of a series
- Divisibility testing
- General algebraic formulae (such as de Moivre's Theorem) and also in calculus, matrices and trigonometry.

These are best illustrated by some worked examples:

Prove that $1 \times 3 + 2 \times 4 + ... + n(n + 2) = \frac{1}{6} n(n + 1)(2n + 7)$

We have to prove the formula for the sum of a series, and we have also been given the nth term of the series. First we show it is true for n = 1.

When $n = 1$, $s_1 = 1 \times 3 = 3$.

The formula gives $1/6 \times 1 \times 2 \times 9 = 3$. So the formula is true for $n = 1$.

Now we must show that if we add the $(k + 1)$th term of the series to s_k we will get the formula for s_{k+1}. It is worth writing this out so that we can see what we are trying to obtain (see right).

$$s_{k+1} = \frac{1}{6} k(k + 1)(2k + 7) + (k + 1)(k + 3)$$

This situation occurs often: take out the fraction and any common factors:

$$s_{k+1} = \frac{1}{6} (k + 1)[k(2k + 7) + (6k + 18)]$$

$$s_{k+1} = \frac{1}{6} (k + 1)(2k^2 + 13k + 18)$$

$$s_{k+1} = \frac{1}{6} (k + 1)(k + 2)(2k + 9) \quad q.e.d.$$

We want to show that:

$$s_{k+1} = \frac{1}{6} (k + 1)(k + 2)(2k + 9)$$

The final line of a proof by induction should always be a statement along the lines of "P(k) true $\Rightarrow$ P(k +1) true by induction, hence the result is true for all $n \in \mathbb{N}$"

In a divisibility test we need to say: "If u_n is divisible by the number, use this fact to show that u_{n+1} is as well."

Prove that $4^n + 6n - 1$ is divisible by 9 for $n \geq 1$.

First prove the result n = 1.

$u_1 = 4 + 6 - 1 = 9$, which is divisible by 9.

If u_k is divisible by 9, then $4^k + 6k - 1 = 9t$ (ie a multiple of 9). We must use this to show that u_{k+1} is also a multiple of 9. Follow these stages – the same technique can be used for every similar question.

$u_{k+1} = 4^{k+1} + 6k + 5$

$4^k + 6k - 1 = 9t$ *(Now multiply by 4 to get 4^{k+1})*

$4^{k+1} + 24k - 4 = 36t$ *(Now subtract 18k to get 6k)*

$4^{k+1} + 6k - 4 = 36t - 18k$ *(Now add 9 to get 5)*

$4^{k+1} + 6k + 5 = 36t - 18k + 9$

So, $u_{k+1} = 9(4t - 2k + 1)$ which is also a multiple of 9

So, if the kth term is divisible by 9, so is the $(k + 1)$th

Other proofs by induction require the appropriate mathematical techniques

---

Prove that $\frac{d}{dx}(x^n) = nx^{n-1}$

When n = 1, the differential of x^1 is 1. The formula gives $1 \times 1^0 = 1$.

How can we use the formula to find the differential of x^{k+1}?

$x^{k+1} = x.x^k$ so we can use the product rule.

$$\frac{d}{dx}(x.x^k) = x.kx^{k-1} + 1.x^k = kx^k + x^k = (k + 1)x^k$$

So we have shown that if the formula is true for x^k, it is also true for x^{k+1}.

We need to show that

$$\frac{d}{dx}(x^{k+1}) = (k + 1)x^k$$

Typically, induction questions are found in section B and therefore you may be asked to extend the answers into other areas such as advanced sequences and series.

a) Prove by mathematical induction that, for $n \in \mathbb{N}$, the sum of the first n integers is given by the formula $n(n + 1)/2$.

When $n = 1$, the sum of the series is 1. The formula gives $1 \times 2 / 2 = 1$. So, true for $n = 1$.
Let $1 + 2 + 3 + \ldots + k = k(k + 1)/2$. We want to show that $1 + 2 + 3 + \ldots + (k + 1) = (k +1)(k + 2)/2$
$$S_{k+1} = \tfrac{1}{2}k(k + 1) + (k + 1) = \tfrac{1}{2}(k + 1)(k + 2)$$

So, if the formula is true for k it is also true for $k + 1$.

b) Find the value of $(1 + 2) + (4 + 5) + (7 + 8) + \ldots + [(3n - 2) + (3n - 1)]$ in terms of n.
When you are asked to find the sum of a "part series", the usual method is to subtract one series from another. In this case, the sum can be calculated as:
$$(1 + 2 + 3 + \ldots + 3n) - (3 + 6 + 9 + \ldots + 3n)$$
(If you are unsure about the use of the 3n in the first series, consider n = 2, for example)

Using the formula in part (a), this works out as $3n(3n + 1)/2 - 3 \times n(n + 1)/2$. Taking out $3n/2$ as a factor we get: $\dfrac{3n}{2}((3n + 1) - (n + 1)) = \dfrac{3n}{2}(2n) = 3n^2$. Always try and verify this sort of answer with a quick substitution. eg: $n = 2$ gives $1 + 2 + 4 + 5 = 12 = 3 \times 2^2$.

YOU SOLVE

a) Write down the first three derivatives of $f(x) = xe^x$
b) Hence suggest a formula for the nth derivative $f^n(x)$ which is true for all $n \in \mathbb{N}$
c) Prove your formula using mathematical induction.

$\underline{xe^x + e^x}$, $\underline{xe^x + 2e^x}$, $\underline{xe^x + 3e^x}$, $\underline{xe^x + ne^x}$

YOU SOLVE

Find the values of S_1, S_2 and S_3 for the series
$$\frac{1}{2} + \frac{1}{6} + \ldots + \frac{1}{n(n + 1)}$$
Suggest a formula for S_n and show by mathematical induction that the formula holds for $n \geq 1$.

$\dfrac{1}{2}, \dfrac{2}{3}, \dfrac{3}{4}, \dfrac{n}{n+1}$ or $1 - \dfrac{1}{n+1}$

Standard formulae: Three standard formulae you should know and should be able to prove using induction are:

$$\sum_{i=1}^{n} i = \tfrac{1}{2}n(n + 1), \qquad \sum_{i=1}^{n} i^2 = \tfrac{1}{6}n(n + 1)(2n + 1)$$

$$\sum_{i=1}^{n} i^3 = \tfrac{1}{4}n^2(n + 1)^2 = (\sum_{i=1}^{n} i)^2$$

Complex Numbers

The square root of –1: The term "imaginary number" is off-putting because it makes the $\sqrt{(-1)}$ seem very abstract. Remember that negative numbers do not exist in real life either: you cannot have a negative amount of anything. As with negative numbers, once $\sqrt{(-1)}$ has been defined, we can fit it into our existing algebra – and very useful it turns out to be.

Definitions: The note box on the right shows the solution of $x^2 + 2x + 5 = 0$. The two solutions, -1 + 2i and -1 – 2i are called *complex numbers* and cannot be further simplified. A complex number z has the form $a + ib$, where a is called the *real part* and b is the *imaginary part*. These can be denoted by Re z and Im z. Note that all real numbers can be considered as complex numbers with a zero imaginary part. The *conjugate*, z^*, of $z = a + ib$ is $a - ib$: thus complex roots of quadratic equations always occur in conjugate pairs.

$$x^2 + 2x + 5 = 0$$
$$x = \frac{-2 \pm \sqrt{4-20}}{2}$$
$$x = \frac{-2 \pm \sqrt{-16}}{2}$$
$$= \frac{-2 \pm 4i}{2} \Rightarrow x = -1 \pm 2i$$

Basic arithmetic: To <u>add</u> complex numbers, add their real parts together, then add their imaginary parts.
- $(a + ib) + (c + id) = (a + c) + i(b + d)$
- Example: $(2 + 3i) + (4 - i) = 6 + 2i$

Your GDC has an i button, so you can do all complex number calculations. Set in complex mode, it will also give complex solutions to equations.

<u>Subtraction</u> is similar:
- $(a + ib) - (c + id) = (a - c) + i(b - d)$
- Example: $(4 + 6i) - (5 + 3i) = -1 + 3i$

<u>Multiplication</u> uses the expansion of brackets:
- $(a + ib) \times (c + id) = ac + iad + ibc + i^2 bd = (ac - bd) + i(ad + bc)$
- Example: $(2 + 4i) \times (2 + 3i) = 4 + 6i + 8i + 12i^2 = -8 + 14i$

Never forget that $i^2 = -1$

One useful fact that follows is that both the addition and multiplication of conjugate pairs give real results.
$$(a + ib) + (a - ib) = 2a \text{ (or } z + z^* = 2\text{Re}(z))$$
$$(a + ib) \times (a - ib) = a^2 - i^2 b^2 = a^2 + b^2 \text{ (or } zz^* = |z|^2)$$

The second result leads to the method for division of complex numbers – similar to the rationalisation of surds.
To <u>divide</u> complex numbers:
- Write the division as a fraction
- Multiply top and bottom by the conjugate of the bottom
- Simplify to the form $a + ib$
- Example: Divide $3 + 2i$ by $1 - 4i$

$$\frac{3 + 2i}{1 - 4i} = \frac{(3 + 2i)(1 + 4i)}{(1 - 4i)(1 + 4i)} = \frac{-5 + 14i}{17} = \frac{-5}{17} + \frac{14}{17}i$$

BEWARE:
The conjugate of $3i$ is $-3i$
The conjugate of 3 is 3
The conjugate of $2i + 1$ is $-2i + 1$
ALWAYS CHANGE THE SIGN OF THE IMAGINARY PART

Equality of complex numbers: If two complex numbers are equal then their real parts can be equated, and their imaginary parts can be equated, often resulting in two equations for the price of one. Use this to solve equations involving complex numbers.

Solve $z^2 = 21 + 20i$, where Re z and Im z are both real numbers.

Writing $z = a + ib$, we get $(a + ib)^2 = 21 + 20i \Rightarrow a^2 - b^2 + 2abi = 21 + 20i$
Equating real and imaginary parts gives $a^2 - b^2 = 21$ and $2ab = 20$.
Substitution leads to the equation $b^4 + 21b^2 - 100 = 0 \Rightarrow (b^2 + 25)(b^2 - 4) = 0$
So $b = \pm 2$ (because it is real), and subbing into $2ab = 20$ gives $a = \pm 5$
So the solutions are: $\underline{z = 5 + 2i \text{ or } -5 - 2i}$

The Complex Plane

Argand diagrams: We can use a *number line* to interpret real numbers geometrically. Each number is represented by a point on the line, or by a position vector - see the number 2 below.

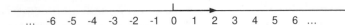

The operation of multiplication by -1 can be represented geometrically by a rotation of 180°. Since $i^2 = -1$, multiplication by i can therefore be represented by a 90° rotation.

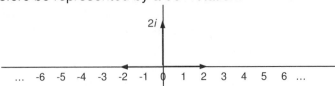

This operation puts $2i$ along a new number line at right angles to the real number line. This is called the *imaginary* axis, and explains why you cannot "see" complex numbers when just operating with real numbers. If we now use the two number lines (real and imaginary) to form two axes, the result is the *complex plane*. Complex numbers can be represented by points or vectors, thus forming *Argand diagrams*.

Magnitude of a complex number: The Argand diagram gives us a way of comparing the size of complex numbers to the size of real numbers. Clearly the numbers 2 and -2 have size (or modulus) 2; this is also the length of their vector representations. The vectors

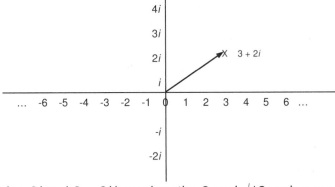

representing $2i$ and $3 + 2i$ have lengths 2 and $\sqrt{13}$: using modulus notation we can write $|3 + 2i| = \sqrt{13}$. In general $|a + ib| = \sqrt{(a^2 + b^2)}$.

Note that $zz^* = |z|^2$

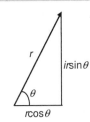

Note that:
- $r \geq 0$
- $-\pi < \theta \leq \pi$

$r\cos\theta + ir\sin\theta$ **form:** Looking at the vector representation above suggests that a complex number could conveniently be written as a length (*modulus*) and angle (*argument*). Thus, $3 + 2i$ has length $\sqrt{13}$ and angle $\tan^{-1}(2/3) \simeq 33.7°$. This can be written in shorthand as $[\sqrt{13}, 33.7°]$. In full, we get $\sqrt{13}\cos33.7° + i\sqrt{13}\sin33.7°$. This form is particularly useful for multiplication and division since:
- $[r, \theta] \times [s, \phi] = [rs, \theta + \phi]$ (*Multiply moduli, add arguments*)
- $[r, \theta] \div [s, \phi] = [r/s, \theta - \phi]$ (*Divide moduli, subtract arguments*)

Note that conversion from $a + ib$ form to $r\cos\theta + ir\sin\theta$ form is the same as converting Cartesian to polar coordinates – make sure you can do this on your calculator (and the reverse as well).

In summary:
- $|a + ib| = \sqrt{(a^2 + b^2)}$
- $\arg(a + ib) = \tan^{-1}(b/a)$
- $\text{Re}[r, \theta] = r\cos\theta$
- $\text{Im}[r, \theta] = r\sin\theta$

Alternative forms for $r\cos\theta + ir\sin\theta$ are $r\text{cis}\theta$ and $re^{i\theta}$. Your calculator may well use the latter, so it is as well to get used to it.

Find the modulus and argument of the complex number $\dfrac{33-i}{10+3i}$

Hint: Either do the division and then find the modulus and argument, or write each number in the shorthand modulus-argument form, and then divide.

$[\sqrt{10}, -18.4°]$

---

a) Write $\dfrac{-1+i}{1+i\sqrt{3}}$ in the form $a + ib$.

b) Express $-1 + i$ and $1 + i\sqrt{3}$ in polar form, and hence the division in (a) in polar form as well.

c) Use your results to show that $\cos 75° = \dfrac{\sqrt{3}-1}{2\sqrt{2}}$

a) $\dfrac{-1+i}{1+i\sqrt{3}} = \dfrac{(-1+i)(1-i\sqrt{3})}{(1+i\sqrt{3})(1-i\sqrt{3})} = \dfrac{(-1+\sqrt{3})+i(1+\sqrt{3})}{4} = \dfrac{-1+\sqrt{3}}{4} + i\dfrac{1+\sqrt{3}}{4}$

b) Using right angled triangles, $-1 + i = [\sqrt{2}, 135°]$, $1 + i\sqrt{3} = [2, 60°]$
So, $[\sqrt{2}, 135°] \div [2, 60°] = [\frac{\sqrt{2}}{2}, 75°]$

c) What has this to do with $\cos 75°$? Well, if the last answer is written in full we get
$\dfrac{\sqrt{2}}{2}\cos 75° + i\dfrac{\sqrt{2}}{2}\sin 75°$ and this equals the division in (a). By equating the real parts of

both divisions we get: $\dfrac{\sqrt{2}}{2}\cos 75° = \dfrac{-1+\sqrt{3}}{4} \Rightarrow \cos 75° = \dfrac{2(-1+\sqrt{3})}{4\sqrt{2}} = \dfrac{\sqrt{3}-1}{2\sqrt{2}}$ q.e.d.

Roots of polynomial equations: How many roots are there to the polynomial equation $P(x) = 0$ if $x \in \mathbb{R}$? If $P(x)$ is a quadratic then there can be either 0 or 2 roots (a repeated root counts as 2). If it's a cubic, there can be 1 or 3, and so on. But if $x \in \mathbb{C}$ then a quadratic will always have 2 (both real or a conjugate pair); a cubic will always have 3 (all real or 1 real and a conjugate pair). In general, a degree n equation has n roots, and any complex roots will always occur in conjugate pairs. Thus, if $2 - 3i$ is a root of $P(x) = 0$, then $2 + 3i$ must be another root.

Example: Find a cubic equation (with real coefficients) which has roots $(2 - i)$ and 3.
The three roots will be 3, $2 - i$ and $2 + i$ so the equation can be written in factor form as $(x - 3)(x - (2 - i))(x - (2 + i)) = 0$
This multiplies out to give $(x - 3)(x^2 - 4x + 5) = 0$ and so the cubic equation is $\underline{x^3 - 7x^2 + 17x - 15 = 0}$

To multiply out the brackets, first remove the inner brackets to get:
$(x - 2 + i)(x - 2 - i)$

Note that the quadratic factor can be found more simply using the fact that the sum of the $(2 - i)$ and $(2 + i)$ is 4, and the product is 5. But this is not specifically in the Higher syllabus.

De Moivre's Theorem

Definition: De Moivre's Theorem gives us a quick way of raising a complex number to any power. To use it, the complex number must be written in polar form. Then:

- $[r, \theta]^n = [r^n, n\theta]$

When written in full, this appears as:

- $(r\cos\theta + ir\sin\theta)^n = r^n\cos n\theta + ir^n\sin n\theta$

It is often used with $r = 1$, in which case:

- $[1, \theta]^n = [1, n\theta]$ or
- $(\cos\theta + i\sin\theta)^n = \cos n\theta + i\sin n\theta$

Applications: One simple use is to find high powers of complex numbers written in $a + ib$ form.

Calculate $(2 + i)^6$.

First convert the number into polar form:	$[\sqrt{5}, 26.6°]^6$
Now apply de Moivre's theorem:	$[125, 159.4°]$
And convert back to a + ib form:	$125\cos 159.4 + i125\sin 159.4$
	$= \mathbf{-117 + 44}\boldsymbol{i}$

But you will find the majority of questions involve finding the roots of complex numbers. First, let's see how we can use de Moivre's theorem to find the roots of 1.

> Using complex numbers, every number will have 2 square roots, 3 cube roots and so on.

Roots of unity: 1 has two square roots, 1 and −1. In the real numbers, it has only one cube root, but we can also find two complex roots. First we write 1 in polar form as $[1, 0°]$, but note that we can also repeatedly add 360° giving:

- $1 = [1, 0°]$ or $[1, 360°]$ or $[1, 720°]$

Now let's form the equation $z^3 = 1$ so that $z = 1^{1/3}$. Thus:

- $z = 1^{1/3} = [1, 0°]^{1/3}$ or $[1, 360°]^{1/3}$ or $[1, 720°]^{1/3}$

Using de Moivre's theorem (which applies to *all* powers), we get:

> The 240° has been rewritten as -120° since the argument is conventionally in the range -180° to 180° .

- $z = [1, 0°]$ or $[1, 120°]$ or $[1, -120°]$

Converting these into $a + ib$ form we find the cube roots of 1 are:

- $1, \; -0.5 + \dfrac{i\sqrt{3}}{2}, \; -0.5 - \dfrac{i\sqrt{3}}{2}$

Note the following points:

- *Each root has magnitude 1, so on an Argand diagram each root is on a circle, radius 1, centre the origin.*
- *If we were to work out the next root in the series we would get 1 again – so there are only 3 roots.*
- *Once we know one root, we could actually find the others by using the symmetry of the Argand diagram.*

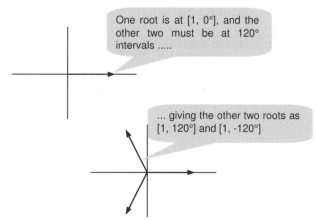

One root is at [1, 0°], and the other two must be at 120° intervals .....

... giving the other two roots as [1, 120°] and [1, -120°]

Roots of complex numbers: The method can now be extended to find the roots of any real or complex number. For example,

---

Find the fifth roots of $1 + i$.

First write $1 + i$ in polar form: $z^5 = 1 + i = [\sqrt{2}, 45°]$

Rearrange: $z = (1 + i)^{1/5} = [\sqrt{2}, 45°]^{1/5}$
$= [2^{1/10}, 9°]$

5 roots, so repeat every 72°   **Roots are:**
$[2^{1/10}, 9°], [2^{1/10}, 81°], [2^{1/10}, 153°], [2^{1/10}, -135°], [2^{1/10}, -63°]$

Convert to $a + ib$ form:
$1.06 + 0.17i, 0.17 + 1.06i, -0.95 + 0.49i, -0.76 - 0.76i, 0.49 - 0.95i$

> Questions involving polar form can equally well ask for calculations in radians (and usually do).

---

a)   **Find the cube roots of 1.**
b)   **Let z = the cube root of 1 in the 2nd quadrant of the complex plane. Evaluate $1 + z + z^2$.**
c)   **Find a given that $|2 + z| = 2|a + z^2|$, a is a real number.**

Work through (c) methodically. First find $2 + z$, then its magnitude. You should get $\sqrt{3}$. Now work through the RHS, and you will eventually get a quadratic equation in a.

YOU SOLVE

(a) 1, $-0.5 + i\sqrt{3}/2$, $-0.5 - i\sqrt{3}/2$ (b) 0   (c) 0.5

Find $|z|$ if $|z + 4| = 2|z + 1|$

Whenever a question involves modulus and argument and the variable z, the best tactic is to rewrite z as $a + ib$. This give us:
$|a + ib + 4| = 2|a + ib + 1|$
Now collect together real and imaginary parts.
$|(a + 4) + ib| = 2|(a + 1) + ib|$
Then we can work out the modulus of each number.
$$\sqrt{(a+4)^2 + b^2} = 2\sqrt{(a+1)^2 + b^2}$$
Squaring both sides:
$(a + 4)^2 + b^2 = 4((a + 1)^2 + b^2)$
Multiplying out and simplifying gives:
$3a^2 + 3b^2 = 12 \Rightarrow a^2 + b^2 = 4$
But the modulus of $z = \sqrt{(a^2 + b^2)}$, so $\underline{|z| = 2}$

This is the sort of question where you don't really know where the answer is going to come from – just start working through and wait to see what happens!

FUNCTIONS AND EQUATIONS

Basics of Functions

A *relation* is an algebraic rule which shows how one set of numbers is related to, or obtained from another set. Relations often model real-life situations, so it is necessary to understand the different types of relation which occur and the notation used.

One-to-one and many-to-one: When two sets of numbers are related, their relationship can be defined in one of four ways:

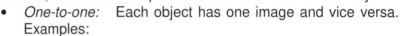

- *One-to-one:* Each object has one image and vice versa. Examples:
  - $x \to x + 1$
  - Name of person $\to$ passport number
- *Many-to-one:* Each object has only one image but different objects can map onto the same image. Examples:
  - $x \to$ nearest integer to x
  - Student $\to$ mark in Math exam
- *One-to-many:* An object can have more than one image but each image is related to only one object. Examples:
  - $x \to \pm\sqrt{x}$
  - Father $\to$ children
- *Many-to-many:* Each object can be related to several images and each image can be related to several objects. Examples:
  - $x \to$ prime factors of x
  - Vegetable $\to$ possible colours of vegetable

Functions are defined as relationships which are either one-to-one or many-to-one.

Defining functions: A function is defined using the notation f: $x \to$... For example, f: $x \to x^2 - 1$. An alternative notation is $f(x) = x^2 - 1$ so that, for example, $f(3) = 3^2 - 1 = 8$. The x value put in to the function is called the *object* and the value of the function which results is called the *image*.

> Read the definition as: "The function f takes any number x and turns it into $x^2 - 1$"

Domain: The set of values to be input to a function is called the *domain* of the function. In many functions, *any* value can be input, in which case the domain is $\mathbb{R}$. However, the domain may be restricted for two reasons:

> Note that a function can also be defined in words:
>
> f: $x \to$ distance from the nearest integer. What is f(2.8) and what is the range?
>
> *The nearest integer to 2.8 is 3, so f(2.8) = 0.2. The distance can never be more than 0.5 so the range is $0 \le x \le 0.5$*

- Certain values of x may give impossible results, such as division by 0 or square root of a negative. For example, the function $f : x \to \dfrac{x}{x-4}$ has the domain restriction $x \ne 4$.
- The domain may be "artificially" restricted. In the following example, the only values of x which are to be input to the function are 3, 4 and 5.

  f: $x \to 2x - 3$, $\{3 \le x \le 5, x \in \mathbb{Z}\}$

The domain (and such restrictions) will always form part of the function definition.

Range: The set of values produced by a function is called the *range*. In the example above, the range would be $3 \le f(x) \le 7$.

Generally, the easiest way to find the range of a function is to look at its graph: the range is the complete set of possible *y* values.

Imagine a "function machine." When the handle is turned, the 5 drops in the top, and the function machine turns it into an 11! This image is used in the next sections.

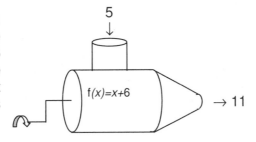

Inverse functions: An inverse function "reverses" the effect of a function. The inverse of add 2 is subtract 2. The inverse of squaring is square rooting. In terms of the function machine, just turn the handle the other way and the 11 turns back into a 5. The notation for an inverse function is $f^{-1}(x)$. A general method for finding inverse functions is as follows:

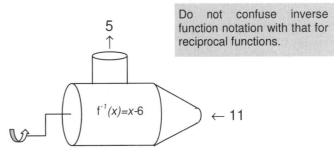

Do not confuse inverse function notation with that for reciprocal functions.

To work out the inverse of a function – particularly a more complex one – the method is:
- Write the function in the form *y* = the function
- Replace the *y* with an *x* and all the *x*'s with *y*'s.
- Make *y* the subject – you will have the inverse function.

Another point to note about inverse functions is that the range of a function becomes the domain of its inverse. Also remember that the graph of $f^{-1}(x)$ is the graph of $f(x)$ reflected in the line *y* = *x*.

Find the inverse function of f: $x \rightarrow \sqrt{(x + 2)}$, $x \geq$ -2. What is the domain of f^{-1}?
(Note the domain restriction which prevents square roots of negative numbers).

$$y = \sqrt{x+2}$$
$$x = \sqrt{y+2}$$
$$x^2 = y + 2$$
$$y = x^2 - 2 \Rightarrow f^{-1}(x) = x^2 - 2$$

The range of the function is $f(x) \geq 0$. So the domain of the inverse function is $x \geq 0$.

Composite functions: If the image numbers from one function are input to another one, the result is a *composite function*. If $f(x) = x^2$ and $g(x) = x - 1$, then $f(g(3)) = f(2) = 4$. Note that this is not the same as $g(f(3)) = g(9) = 8$. It is important to understand that the functions are not being multiplied together – a number is being put through one function, then the other. This can be illustrated using two function machines.

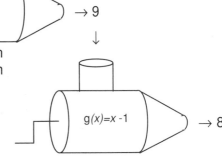

To avoid multiple brackets in g(f(3)), the actual notation used is (g ∘ f)(3). Say this as "g of f of 3" and remember that 3 is put into f first and then into g.

To find (g ∘ f)(x), work like this:

g(f(x)) = g(x^2)   Now function g in words is "subtract 1", so we end up with $x^2 - 1$.   Similarly, (f ∘ g)(x) = f(x − 1). Function f is "square" so we end up with $(x - 1)^2$.

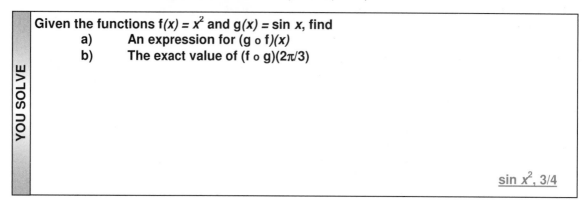

YOU SOLVE

Given the functions f(x) = x^2 and g(x) = sin x, find
   a)   **An expression for (g ∘ f)(x)**
   b)   **The exact value of (f ∘ g)(2π/3)**

<u>sin x^2, 3/4</u>

The inverse of a many-to-one function: The inverse of a one-to-one function is itself one-to-one and therefore also a function. However, the inverse of a many-to-one is a one-to-many and hence *not* a function, unless the domain of the original is restricted, hence turning it into a one-to-one function.

For example, the graph shows a quadratic with a vertex at x = -2.

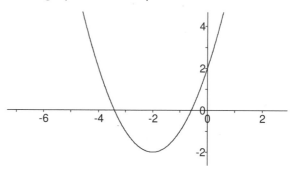

There are no domain restrictions. However, if the inverse is to be a function, we must restrict the domain of the quadratic to remove the turning point. So, a suitable restriction would be x ≥ -2. When reflected in the line y = x (to get the graph of the inverse function) the result is:

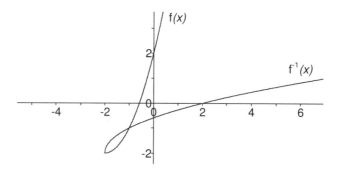

The inverse is a function since it is a one-to-one relationship.

Graphs of Functions

A graph is an excellent tool for interpreting a function. From a graph we can see when the function is increasing or decreasing, what the range of the function is, where it cuts the axes and so on. Therefore it is important to be able to sketch and understand graphs of different types of functions. Remember that your calculator can be of great benefit, and you should fully understand its graphing functions (see page 25).

Domain and range on a graph:

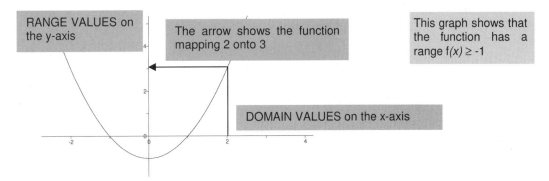

RANGE VALUES on the y-axis

The arrow shows the function mapping 2 onto 3

This graph shows that the function has a range $f(x) \geq -1$

DOMAIN VALUES on the x-axis

Graphing terms:

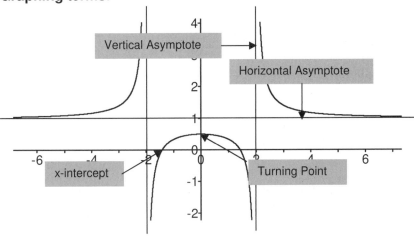

Vertical Asymptote

Horizontal Asymptote

x-intercept

Turning Point

- The vertical asymptote is caused by *x*-values for which the function would be undefined (ie domain restrictions)
- The horizontal asymptote represents the value that the function tends to for very large *x*-values (both positive and negative)
- Turning points can be maximums or minimums. At these points the gradient of the graph is zero.
- *x*- and *y*-intercepts can be calculated by setting (respectively) the *y* and *x* values in the function to 0.

Transformations of graphs: You should be able to sketch the graphs of the basic functions $y = x^2$, $y = x^3$, $y = 1/x$, $y = a^x$, $y = \log x$. The effect of simple numerical changes to these functions (involving additions, multiplications and minus signs) results in specific, simple transformations, thus extending the number of functions which can be easily sketched.

The graph transformations you need to know are:

Change to function	Transformation
$y = f(x) + a$	Move graph upwards by a units
$y = f(x + a)$	Move graph to the *left* by a units
$y = af(x)$	Stretch graph vertically by scale factor a
$y = f(ax)$	Stretch graph horizontally by scale factor $1/a$
$y = -f(x)$	Reflect graph in x-axis
$y = f(-x)$	Reflect graph in y-axis

Remember: transformations in the x direction always do the opposite of what you expect!

For example, $y = (x - 1)^2 + 2$ will move the graph of $y = x^2$ to the right by 1 and up by 2, that is, a translation of $\begin{pmatrix} 1 \\ 2 \end{pmatrix}$

$y = -\dfrac{3}{x + 2}$ is a multiple transformation of $y = \dfrac{1}{x}$. To obtain the correct order of transformations, consider what order you would work out the expression if you put in a value for x. This would be:

- Add 2 to x
- Multiply the function by 3
- Change sign

The equivalent transformations are:

- Move left 2 units
- Stretch by 3 in the y direction
- Reflect in the x-axis

Be aware of the difference between, say, adding 2 to the x part of the function, and adding 2 to the *whole* function.

The graph of $f^{-1}(x)$: Consider the graph of $y = x^2$, $x \geq 0$, (which represents the function $f(x) = x^2$). When $x = 3$, $y = 9$ (ie $f(3) = 9$). The graph of the inverse function is $y = \sqrt{x}$, and when $x = 9$, $y = 3$. *Any* point (a, b) on the graph of $f(x)$ becomes (b, a) on the graph of $f^{-1}(x)$. This represents a reflection in the line $y = x$.

- The graph of $f^{-1}(x)$ is always the graph of $f(x)$ reflected in the line $y = x$.

Absolute value function: The graph of $|f(x)|$ is simple to sketch once you have the graph of $f(x)$: the positive parts of the graph (ie above the x-axis) remain the same, the negative parts are reflected in the x-axis.

The graph of $f(|x|)$ works slightly differently. Draw it as follows:
- Draw the graph of $f(x)$ but only for $x \geq 0$.
- Reflect this section in the y-axis.
- The two sections together make up the graph of $y = f(|x|)$

Reciprocal of $f(x)$: Drawing the graph of $\dfrac{1}{f(x)}$ from the graph of $f(x)$ takes slightly more skill. Work as follows:
- All points with a y-coordinate of 1 or -1 remain in the same place.
- Any vertical asymptotes (discontinuities) become points on the x-axis, the x-coordinate remaining the same.
- Any points on the x-axis become discontinuities.
- The rest of the graph is completed by ensuring that values for
  $0 < y < 1$ become >1, and for $-1 < y < 0$ become < -1.
- Also note that $f(x)$ and its reciprocal always have the same sign.

Both modulus and reciprocal can be easily drawn using your calculator, (as long as the coefficients are numeric).

The graph of $y = f(x)$ has a vertical asymptote at $x = 1$, a point of inflexion at (0,0) and a maximum at (1.5,-0.675). Sketch the graphs of $y = 1/f(x)$, $y = |f(x)|$ and $y = f(|x|)$.

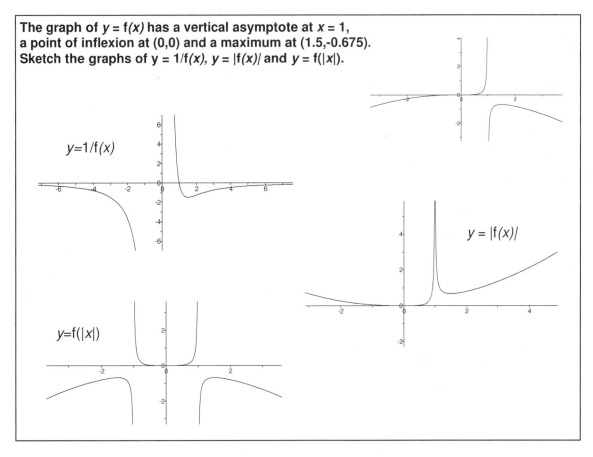

$y=1/f(x)$

$y = |f(x)|$

$y=f(|x|)$

Using a GDC: Your calculator is an essential tool especially when dealing with functions and graphs. Not only can you use it to check answers worked out "by hand", but you can use it to solve equations, find turning points and areas under curves and so on. Some questions can *only* be answered using the GDC.

Tables: GDCs have a facility to work out a table of values for a function. Having input the function in the form $y = f(x)$ you can set up a table by selecting the first x value and then the steps by which you want x to increase. In this example, the function $y = 2 - 3\sin x$ has been entered into the function editor, and then a table created starting with $x = 0$ and increasing x in steps of 30. This can be helpful if you need to know several values, if you want to plot a graph by hand or if you're having difficulty creating the appropriate scales for a calculator plot – the table indicates the lowest and highest values of y.

Drawing graphs: Three important points to remember when drawing and using GDC graphs.

- Make sure the function you type into the editor is actually the same as in the question. You may, for example, have to use brackets which aren't actually required on the written page. $2^{x + 3}$, if typed as 2 ^ x + 3, will work out values of $2^x + 3$. You need a bracket: 2 ^ $(x + 3)$
- The GDC has a few standard sets of scales, but you will probably have to set up the "window" yourself in order to see the required part of the graph. You may well have to zoom into a part of the graph to see exactly what is happening. The two screenshots on the right are of the same graph, but only the lower one shows the intersections with the x-axis.

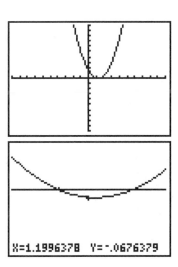

• The GDC can give you the values of key points such as intersections with the axes, points where lines intersect, turning points and so on. If you want to read off your own point, make sure you know the scales being used, ie how much each mark on the axes is worth.

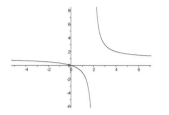

Vertical asymptotes: The graph of $y = \dfrac{x}{x-2}$ (left) has a vertical asymptote at $x = 2$, but the GDC may not display it very well; some calculators will "join up" the two parts of the graph. You can overcome this by using "dot" instead of "connected" mode; but do be aware of this limitation.

Solving equations: GDCs have built in equation solvers. They can sometimes be a little cumbersome to use, so it is probably better to use graphs to solve equations. The easiest way to do this is to ensure your equation has a 0 on the right hand side because then all you have to do is find out where the graph cuts the axis.

Can you input these functions into your GDC?
$\sqrt[3]{x}$, $|x|$, $\sin^2 x$

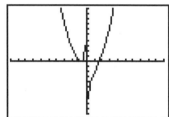

For example, solve $x^2 - 2 = \dfrac{1}{x}$, $x > 0$.

First we need to rewrite this equation as $x^2 - 2 - \dfrac{1}{x} = 0$. The graph is shown on the left.

Now use the "zero" or "root" feature to find where the graph cuts the x-axis and this will be the solution to the equation. $x = 1.618$

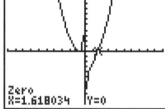

Zero
X=1.618034   Y=0

YOU SOLVE

$f(x) = x^3 \times 2^{-x}$, $x \geq 0$.

a) **Sketch the graph of f(x), showing its asymptotic behaviour.**
 Note the domain of the function.

b) **Find the co-ordinates of the maximum point, and hence state the range of f(x).**
 Once you know the y-coordinate of the maximum, you can use this to write down the range. Again, note the domain.

c) **Draw a line on your graph to show that f(x) = 1 has two solutions.**

d) **Find the solutions to f(x) = 1, giving your answers to 3 significant figures.**
 Either draw y = 1 on your calculator and find the two points of intersection, or draw the graph of $y = x^3 \times 2^{-x} - 1$ and find where it intersects the x axis.

Maximum = (4.33, 4.04), Range is $0 \leq f(x) \leq 4.04$, x = 1.37 or 9.94

Reciprocal Functions

In the reciprocal function $f(x) = \dfrac{a}{x}$, where a is a constant, the function *decreases* as the x values increase. Specifically, if an x value is multiplied by any number, the y value will be divided by the same number.

Example: The time taken to fly a fixed distance against the speed. (If the speed doubles, the time halves).

Graph: The diagram shows the graphs of two reciprocal functions. They have similar shapes. Each graph is in two sections, with the y-axis being a vertical asymptote. Since they are also self-reflections about $y = x$ this means that a reciprocal function is its own inverse. For example $f(x) = \dfrac{12}{x} \Rightarrow f^{-1}(x) = \dfrac{12}{x}$.

This is easily seen if 2 is put into the function: $\dfrac{12}{2} = 6$ then $\dfrac{12}{6} = 2$.

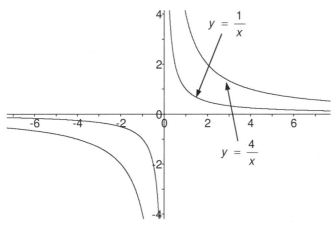

If f(x) = 2/(x-1),

a)   State the transformations which will transform the graph of $y = 1/x$ into the graph of $y = f(x)$

b)   Hence sketch the graph of $y = |f(x)|$

c)   What will the domain and range of the function $g(x) = |f(x)| + 2$ be?

a)   The 1 has been subtracted from the x, so the graph is first translated forward 1 parallel to the x-axis. (Remember that the direction is always opposite to what you would expect in the x-direction). The second transformation is a stretch ×2 parallel to the y-axis.

b)   Carry out the transformations in (a), then reflect any negative values in the x-axis. Put $x = 0$ to check where the graph intersects the y-axis.

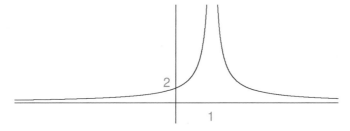

c)   The graph will now be shifted up 2. By considering this new graph, we can work out that the domain is $x \neq 1$. The range will be $g(x) > 2$.

Quadratic Functions

Quadratic functions occur in many different situations. You should be completely familiar with the connections between the functions and their graphs, and with the methods for solving quadratic equations.

Equation: $f(x) = ax^2 + bx + c$

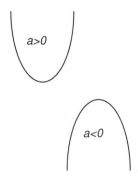

Graph: All quadratic graphs are parabolas, the sign of a determining "which way up." In the form shown above, we can say which way up the graph is and where the y-intercept is. For example, the graph of $y = x^2 + 3x - 4$ cuts the y-axis at (0, -4) and is in the shape of a U. The graph is always symmetrical about the vertical line passing through the vertex (turning point), a fact which can often be used when answering questions about the graph. This line has equation $x = -\dfrac{b}{2a}$.

Factorisation: Quadratics come in different forms:

- $ax^2 + bx = x(ax + b)$ eg: $2x^2 - 6x = 2x(x - 3)$
- $x^2 - a^2 = (x - a)(x + a)$ eg: $x^2 - 49 = (x - 7)(x + 7)$
- When all three terms of a quadratic are present, if it factorises, it will factorise into two brackets. Look for two numbers which multiply to give c and add to give b.
  $x^2 - 3x - 4 = (x - 4)(x + 1)$ (Because $-4 \times 1 = -4$, $-4 + 1 = -3$)
- If $a \neq 1$, first take out the number multiplying x^2 as a factor.
  $2x^2 - 14x + 24 = 2(x^2 - 7x + 12) = 2(x - 4)(x - 3)$

In its factorised form, the equation reveals more information about the graph. If the equation factorises to $(x - p)(x - q)$ then the points $(p, 0)$ and $(q, 0)$ are the x-intercepts – ie the values of x where the function equals zero.

> In the last case, if a cannot be taken out as a factor, factorise by inspection. Or use the method which starts "look for two numbers which multiply to give ac and add to give b".

Completing the square: This method gives us a third form of the quadratic function. Method and example are shown below.

1. For $x^2 + bx + c$ start by writing $(x + d)^2$ where $d = b \div 2$.	$x^2 + 6x + 7$ $(x + 3)^2$ ....
2. Now write down $-d^2$.	$(x + 3)^2 - 9$ ....
3. Write down c and simplify.	$(x + 3)^2 - 9 + 7$ $= \underline{\mathbf{(x + 3)^2 - 2}}$
For quadratics where $a \neq 1$, start by taking a out as a common factor. Forget about it whilst completing the square. Multiply it back at the end.	$2x^2 - 6x - 4$ $= 2(x^2 - 3x - 2)$ $= 2[(x - 1.5)^2 - 2.25 - 2]$ $= 2[(x - 1.5)^2 - 4.25]$ $= \underline{\mathbf{2(x - 1.5)^2 - 8.5}}$

In this form, the function can be seen to be a transformation of $y = x^2$. In the first example above, the transformation is a translation of $\begin{pmatrix} -3 \\ -2 \end{pmatrix}$. Since the vertex of $y = x^2$ is (0, 0), the vertex of the new quadratic will be (-3, -2). In general, the completed square form is always:

$f(x) = a(x - h)^2 + k$ and this gives a vertex of (h, k).

Solving Quadratic Equations

Except for the simplest form of quadratic equation shown on the right the first move is always collect together terms on the left with 0 on the right.

$x^2 = 25$
$x = \pm 5$

Factorisation: If the quadratic expression factorises, this is the simplest method of solution. Make sure you understand the connection between the factors and the *x*-intercepts (see previous section) since questions can link the equation to the graph.

Example: Solve the equation
$2x^2 - 4x = x^2 - 3$

$x^2 - 4x + 3 = 0$
$(x - 3)(x - 1) = 0$
$x = 3 \text{ or } 1$

Formula: *All* quadratics can be solved using the formula, although it is most useful when the expression does not factorise.

The solution of $ax^2 + bx + c$ is: $x = \dfrac{-b \pm \sqrt{b^2 - 4ac}}{2a}$. It is the $\pm$ which leads to the two possible solutions. Make sure that you can use your calculator to find both solutions quickly. (As well as a straight calculation, you can use a program or use the equation solver).

Example: Solve the equation
$2x^2 - 4x = x + 2$

$2x^2 - 5x - 2 = 0$

$x = \dfrac{-(-5) \pm \sqrt{(-5)^2 - 4 \times 2 \times (-2)}}{2 \times 2}$

$x = \dfrac{5 \pm \sqrt{41}}{4}$

$\therefore x = 2.851, -0.351$

Be careful to substitute correctly, particularly when there are minus signs around. Follow the example on the right carefully.

The solutions to a quadratic equation are the points where the graph crosses the *x*-axis. This can lead to 0, 1 or 2 solutions. These correspond to values of $b^2 - 4ac$ which are <0, $=0$ and >0 respectively. $b^2 - 4ac$ is called the *discriminant* since it discriminates between the number of solutions.

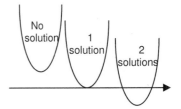

Find the range of values of *p* for which $x^2 - px + (p + 3) > 0$ for all real *x*.

Look at the small sketches above: a quadratic function with all positive values has no solutions, so its discriminant is negative.

So, $(-p)^2 - 4(p + 3) < 0 \Rightarrow p^2 - 4p - 12 < 0$

This is a quadratic inequality (see page 30) which is solved by finding the critical values (ie which give 0).

$(p - 6)(p + 2) < 0$ has critical values $p = 6$ and $p = -2$

We want the values of *p* to be less than 0 so $\underline{-2 < p < 6.}$

The function $f(x) = r + qx - px^2$ has the graph shown.

a) How many solutions are there to the equation
$r + qx = px^2$?

b) Show that $q^2 + 4pr > 0$ and hence find the minimum value of *r* if $q = 4$ and $p = 2$.

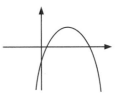

a) <u>2</u>   b) <u>*r* > -2</u>

Inequalities

Linear inequalities: Linear inequalities are solved in exactly the same way as equations except for one important difference:

- When multiplying or dividing by a negative number, the inequality sign must be turned round.

eg:
$$8 - 2x > 4$$
$$-2x > -4$$
$$x < 2$$

One way to avoid this is to move the x term to the other side:
$$8 - 2x > 4$$
$$8 > 4 + 2x$$
$$4 > 2x$$
$$2 > x \quad \text{(ie: } x < 2 \text{ as before)}$$

> Remember that you can only use the double inequality when x lies in a single range. When x lies in one of two possible ranges, use two inequalities.

Quadratic inequalities: Remember that if $x^2 < 4$, then it follows that $-2 < x < 2$. And if $x^2 > 4$, $x > 2$ or $x < -2$. Quadratic inequalities will always result in ranges such as this. In more complicated ones, factorise first:

eg:
$$x^2 - 3x - 18 < 0$$
$$(x - 6)(x + 3) < 0$$
$$\text{So } -3 < x < 6 \quad \text{(it is helpful to consider the graph).}$$

Inequalities involving the modulus function: If $|x| < 3$ then it follows that $-3 < x < 3$. Using this, we can solve:
$$|2x - 1| < 3$$
$$-3 < 2x - 1 < 3$$
$$-2 < 2x < 4 \quad \text{(Add 1 to each of the three parts)}$$
$$-1 < x < 2 \quad \text{(Divide each part by 2)}$$

There are other ways of solving this inequality;
- Square both sides to remove the absolute value sign, then solve as a quadratic inequality.
- Draw the graph of $y = |2x - 1|$ and see for which values of x the graph lies below 3.

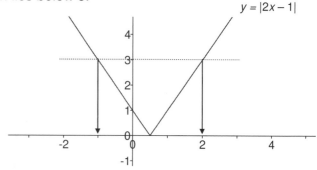

$y = |2x - 1|$

Inequalities involving rational expressions: There are problems when we try to solve the inequality $\dfrac{2}{x - 2} > \dfrac{1}{x - 3}$. Normally we would multiply by $x - 3$ and by $x - 2$ to remove the bottom lines, but we don't know whether these terms are positive or negative. Hence, we don't know whether or not we should reverse the inequality sign. There are two methods of solution, the first being graphically (and therefore GDC) orientated, the second algebraic. These methods are illustrated on the next page.

Method 1:   In this method we draw the graph of each inequality and read off the values of x for which the inequality is satisfied.

The solution can be read off the graph directly as $2 < x < 3$ or $x > 4$ since these are the regions where the graph of $y = \dfrac{2}{x-2}$ is above the graph of $y = \dfrac{1}{x-3}$.

This is actually quite hard to see on the calculator, so ....

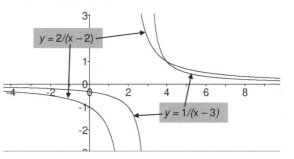

Method 2:   We can move everything to the left hand side and then write as a single fraction:

$$\frac{2}{x-2} > \frac{1}{x-3}$$

$$\frac{2}{x-2} - \frac{1}{x-3} > 0$$

$$\frac{2(x-3) - 1(x-2)}{(x-2)(x-3)} > 0$$

$$\frac{x-4}{(x-2)(x-3)} > 0$$

Now the critical values where the fraction will experience a change of sign are 2, 3 and 4. A sign diagram will help us to see when the value of the fraction is positive.

x		2		3		4	
Fraction	<0		>0		<0		>0

So the solution is $2 < x < 3$, or $x > 4$

Find the values of x for which $x - 2 > 3/x$

YOU SOLVE

$-1 < x < 0$ or $x > 3$

Find the values of x for which $\dfrac{3}{x+1} < \dfrac{2}{x}$

YOU SOLVE

$x < -1$ or $0 < x < 2$

Polynomial Functions

Polynomials are of the form $a_nx^n + a_{n-1}x^{n-1} + ... + a_1x + a_0$ and are easy to deal with. Differentiation and integration, for example, are a piece of cake. When polynomials factorise this leads to the easy solution of polynomial equations.

The *degree* of a polynomial is the highest power of x.

The factor theorem: There is a set routine for factorising a quadratic. For any higher degree polynomial, we can test possible factors using the factor theorem. This states that, for a polynomial function f(x), $(x - a)$ is a factor if f(a) = 0.

If we were testing $x + 2$, then we would work out f(-2)

eg: Show that $(x - 2)$ is a factor of f(x) = $x^3 - 3x^2 - 2x + 8$.
f(2) = $2^3 - 3 \times 2^2 - 2 \times 2 + 8$ = 0, so (x – 2) is a factor

Once we know a factor we can divide it into the polynomial to find the other factors. Compare this with numbers – suppose we want the factors of 30 and know that 5 is one of them:

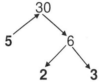

Thus the prime factors of 30 are 2, 3 and 5

How do we do polynomial division? One way is the full long division method, another is by inspection. A useful in-between method is called *synthetic division*. With this method we only need to use numbers: in the example above these will be the 2 from the $x - 2$ and the coefficients of the polynomial, 1, -3, -2 and 8.

Stage 1:   Lay out the numbers as on the right – including the 0 under the first coefficient.

2	1	-3	-2	8
	0			

Stage 2:   Add the first column, multiply the result by the 2 and put the answer in the second column. Continue along the columns.

2	1	-3	-2	8
	0	2	-2	-8
	1	-1	-4	0

Stage 3:   The 0 is the remainder – this will always be 0 when we divide by a factor. The other numbers in the bottom row are the coefficients of the second factor: in this case, $x^2 - x - 4$. Thus, we know that: $(x - 2)(x^2 - x - 4) = x^3 - 3x^2 - 2x + 8$

The quadratic will not yield any rational factors so that's as far as we can go in this case.

The remainder theorem: If $(x - a)$ is not a factor of polynomial f(x) then it will leave a remainder when f(x) is divided by $(x - a)$. This remainder can be calculated as f(a).

Thus the factor theorem is really just a special case of the remainder theorem – a factor leads to a remainder of 0.

eg: What is the remainder when $x^3 - 3x + 1$ is divided by $(x + 2)$?
Putting –2 into the polynomial gives $(-2)^3 - 3 \times (-2) + 1$ = -1. So the remainder is –1.
Note that if you had used synthetic division instead, the final number at the bottom right would be the remainder, -1. And you would put a 0 in the top row for the $0x^2$ term.

Solution of polynomial equations: How many real solutions does $f(x) = 0$ have if $f(x)$ is a cubic function? If the graph has two turning points, there are three possibilities:

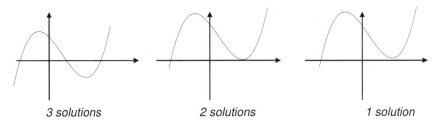

| 3 solutions | 2 solutions | 1 solution |

These geometric configurations have algebraic equivalents which can be seen when the polynomial has been fully factorised:

- 3 solutions from three distinct linear factors
  eg: $(x - 4)(x - 2)(x + 1) = 0$ *has solutions 4, 2 and -1.*
- 2 solutions from one linear factor and one "repeated" factor
  eg: $(x + 3)(x - 1)^2 = 0$ *has solutions -3 and 1. The repeated factor is the "touch" on the axis as opposed to the "cut."*
- 1 solution from one linear one irreducible quadratic factor
  eg: $(x + 2)(x^2 + x + 1) = 0$ *has solution x = -2*

If we allow complex solutions then the 1 real solution becomes 1 real and a complex conjugate pair (from the quadratic).

Show that $x = 1$ is a solution of the equation $2x^3 - x^2 + 8 = 7x + 2$, and find any further solutions.

The first part is a matter of simple substitution, but you must ensure that you *show* the result.

$\underline{2 \times 1^3 - 1^2 + 8 = 9 \text{ and } 7 \times 1 + 2 = 9. \text{ So } x = 1 \text{ is a solution.}}$

Now we have a cubic equation to solve, so everything to the left hand side.
$$2x^3 - x^2 - 7x + 6 = 0$$
We know $x = 1$ is a solution, so $(x - 1)$ is a factor. Now we divide by this factor:

1	2	-1	-7	6
	0	2	1	-6
	2	1	-6	0

So the quadratic factor is $2x^2 + x - 6$. This factorises to give $(2x - 3)(x + 2)$. Thus the remaining two solutions are $\underline{1.5}$ and $\underline{-2}$.

The function $f(x) = x^3 + ax^2 - 2x + b$ has $(x + 1)$ as a factor, and leaves a remainder of -3 when divided by $x - 2$. Find the values of a and b.
Use the factor theorem and then the remainder theorem to form two equations in a and b.

$\underline{a = -2}, \quad \underline{b = 1}$

YOU SOLVE

Suggest an equation for the curve shown in the diagram.
As well as the x-intercepts, look at the y-intercept and which way up the graph is.

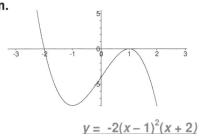

$\underline{y = -2(x - 1)^2(x + 2)}$

YOU SOLVE

Exponential and Logarithmic Functions

Equations: $f(x) = a^x, \ x \in \mathbb{Q}, \ a > 0$

$f(x) = \log_a x, \ x > 0, \ a > 0$

Notice the domains. In particular, it is not possible to find the logarithm of a negative number.

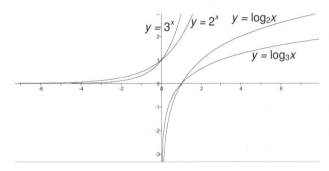

Graphs: In the same way that all quadratics have the same shape, all exponential curves and all logarithmic curves are pretty much the same. The diagram shows $y = 2^x$, $y = 3^x$, $y = \log_2 x$ and $y = \log_3 x$. Note that the log functions are the inverses of the exponential functions, so their graphs are reflections of each other in the line $y = x$.

Questions draw on your knowledge of the laws of indices and logarithms. You should also be familiar with the following rules:

- If $a^x = b$, then $x = \log_a b$ (eg: $2^3 = 8$, so $\log_2 8 = 3$)
- $x = \log_a a^x$ (This is similar to $x = \sqrt{x^2}$)
- $x = a^{\log_a x}$ (This is similar to $x = (\sqrt{x})^2$)

e^x and $\ln x$: The number e is, like π, given a letter because it is irrational and hence impossible to write accurately using decimals. It is approximately 2.718. The functions e^x and e^{-x} are important because they are used to model situations where the rate of growth or decay of the quantity x is dependent on the value of x at any time. Typical applications are population growth and radioactive decay. $\ln x$ is the inverse of e^x and is short for $\log_e x$.

For the function f(x) = ln($2x^2 - 5x - 3$), find
a)   **The domain of f(x), giving your answers exactly;**
b)   **The range of x.**

a)   Draw the graph on your calculator, and you will see the graph has no central section. You need to find these two vertical asymptotes, and these will be the values of x which give ln(0). So we need to solve the quadratic $2x^2 - 5x - 3 = 0$. This factorises as $(2x + 1)(x - 3) = 0$ leading to solutions $x = -0.5$ and 3. From the graph, the domain of x is thus __$x \leq -0.5$ or $x \geq 3$__

b)   log graphs generally have a range spanning all real numbers, and this can be seen from your calculator display. Thus, __f(x) $\in$ R__

A group of ten monkeys is introduced to a zoo. After t years the number of monkeys, N, is modelled by $N = 10e^{0.3t}$.
a)   **How many monkeys are there after 2 years?**
b)   **How long will it take for the number of monkeys to reach 50?**

__18 monkeys__ ,   __5.36 years__ or say __about 6 years.__

YOU SOLVE

Find the domain of the function f(x) = $\sqrt{\ln(x - 3)}$

The easiest way is to draw the graph on your calculator then see what x values are possible. But try to justify it algebraically as well.

__$x \geq 4$__

YOU SOLVE

CIRCULAR FUNCTIONS AND TRIGONOMETRY

Definitions and Formulae

Radians: Radians are an alternative to degrees when measuring the size of angles. Although it is easier to *think* in degrees, radians are often used with trigonometric functions and *must* be used when differentiating or integrating them.

- The conversion is π radians = 180°. (Note that an angle is assumed to be in radians unless the degrees symbol is given).

It is worth memorising some key angles in radians (see table on the right). π appears in many angles when expressed in radians (because of the conversion) but it does not have to. For example, 45° = 0.785..., but this is not an *exact* conversion, unlike $\pi/4$.

There are two circle formulae which are used when a sector angle is expressed in radians. If the angle is θ and the radius of the circle is r:

- Arc length of sector = $r\theta$
- Area of sector = $\frac{1}{2}r^2\theta$

30° = $\pi/6$
45° = $\pi/4$
60° = $\pi/3$
90° = $\pi/2$
120° = $2\pi/3$
180° = π
270° = $3\pi/2$
360° = 2π

The diagram shows two concentric circles with radii 1 and 4.
If AOB = $\pi/3$, find
a)   The area of ABCD
b)   The perimeter of ABCD

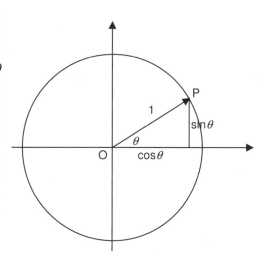

AOB is in radians. The area of sector AOB = $\frac{1}{2}r^2\theta = \frac{1}{2} \times 4^2 \times \pi/3$
Similarly, sector DOC has area $\frac{1}{2} \times 1^2 \times \pi/3$
Subtracting, area ABCD = $8\pi/3 - 0.5\pi/3$ = **7.85**

For the perimeter, AD = BC = 3. Arc AB = $r\theta = 4 \times \pi/3$, and arc CD = $1 \times \pi/3$. So, total is: $3 + 3 + 4\pi/3 + \pi/3 =$ **11.24**

Trigonometric functions:

The diagram shows a circle with radius 1 (a *unit circle*). A line is drawn from the centre O to a point P on the circumference, and this forms angle θ with the positive *x*-axis. Then the *x*-coordinate of the point is defined as the cosine of the angle ($\cos\theta$) and the *y*-coordinate as the sine ($\sin\theta$). These definitions will apply as the line rotates full circle, giving the sin and cos for all angles from 0° to 360°. When these are plotted as graphs, we get the following:

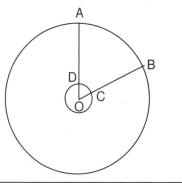

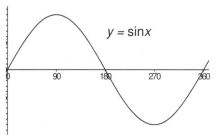

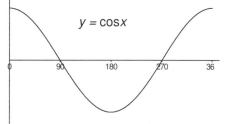

These graphs can, of course, be extended to show the sin and cos for *all* angles.

Points to note:
- The range of both functions is $-1 \leq f(x) \leq 1$
- $\sin x > 0$ for angles between 0° and 180°
- $\cos x > 0$ for angles between 0° and 90°, also between 270° and 360°
- Both functions have a *period* (ie repeat themselves) every 360°.

Exact values: You are expected to know the exact values of the sin, cos and tan of multiples of 30° and multiples of 45°. Learn the table on the right by heart:

	0°	30°	45°	60°	90°
sin	0	$\frac{1}{2}$	$\frac{\sqrt{2}}{2}$	$\frac{\sqrt{3}}{2}$	1
cos	1	$\frac{\sqrt{3}}{2}$	$\frac{\sqrt{2}}{2}$	$\frac{1}{2}$	0
tan	0	$\frac{1}{\sqrt{3}}$	1	$\sqrt{3}$	∞

> Note that the top row is the same as:
> $$\frac{\sqrt{0}}{2}, \frac{\sqrt{1}}{2}, \frac{\sqrt{2}}{2}, \frac{\sqrt{3}}{2}, \frac{\sqrt{4}}{2}$$
> - a useful *aide-memoire*

The sin and cos of further multiples can be deduced from the symmetries of the graphs. eg: $\cos 225° = -\frac{\sqrt{2}}{2}$, $\sin 330° = -\frac{1}{2}$.

The tan function simply repeats every 180°, so $\tan 240° = \sqrt{3}$.

Simple trigonometric equations: $\sin\theta = 0.4$, $0° \leq \theta \leq 360°$. What is the value of θ? We want to know what angle has a sin which is 0.4. Using the sine inverse function (written as $\sin^{-1}$ or arcsin) on your calculator, we find θ is 23.6°. Using the symmetry of the sin graph above, another solution is $180 - 23.6 = 156.4°$. (If the domain is in radians, you can either work in degrees and convert at the end, or set your calculator to radians: this gives $\theta = 0.412$, and the second solution is $\pi - 0.411 = 2.73$).

> Another example: Solve
> $\cos(\theta - 30) = 0.2$, $0° \leq \theta \leq 360°$
>
> $\cos^{-1}(0.2) = 78.5°$ or $281.5°$
> So $\theta - 30 = 78.5$ or 281.5
> $\theta = 108.5°$ or $311.5°$

Finding cos and tan from sin: A simple trick is to draw a right-angled triangle. If $\sin\theta = \frac{3}{5}$, what is $\cos\theta$?

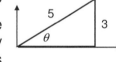

Having put 3 as the "opposite" and 5 as the hypoteneuse, the remaining side must be 4 (by Pythagoras). So $\cos\theta = \frac{4}{5}$ and $\tan\theta = \frac{3}{4}$. If θ was obtuse, $\cos\theta$ would be $-\frac{4}{5}$.

More trig functions and inverses:

$\tan\theta$ is calculated as $\frac{\sin\theta}{\cos\theta}$ and has period π.

Each of sin, cos and tan has a reciprocal function. The periods of these functions are the same as the functions they are linked to.

$\sec\theta$ is the reciprocal of $\cos\theta$ ("sec" is short for "secant")

$\text{cosec}\,\theta$ is the reciprocal of $\sin\theta$ ("cosec" is short for "cosecant")

$\cot\theta$ is the reciprocal of $\tan\theta$ ("cot" is short for "cotangent")

> The third letter of each of the reciprocal functions tells you to which function it is linked.
> se**c** with **c**os
> cose**c** with **s**in
> cota**n** with **t**an

You must also know about the inverses of sin, cos and tan, not just for their use in solving equations but as functions in their own right. The inverse of sinx, for example, is written as $\sin^{-1}x$ or arcsinx.

Simplify $\dfrac{\cos^2\theta\,\sec\theta}{\sin\theta}$.

The best way to deal with these functions is to convert everything to sin and cos. So:

$$\frac{\cos^2\theta\,\sec\theta}{\sin\theta} = \frac{\cos^2\theta \times \dfrac{1}{\cos\theta}}{\sin\theta} = \frac{\cos\theta}{\sin\theta} = \cot\theta$$

Domain and range: You need to know the domain and range of all these functions. The range of the inverses is restricted to ensure that they are functions and this leads to the idea of *principal values*. When finding the inverse sin of an angle, the principal value will be an angle between -90° and 90°; for inverse cos, it will be between 0° and 180°. These are the values you will obtain on your calculator. The table below shows all the domains and ranges, and the graphs follow. Compare tables and graphs. Note that questions are not often set which just test this knowledge: it is more likely that your understanding of trig.

functions is used in more complex problems. ▤ It is really *most* important that your calculator is set to radians or degrees as appropriate. Get into the habit of checking *first* before attempting any question involving trigonometric functions. Questions will be set in radians unless degrees are specifically mentioned.

Domains, Ranges and Graphs:

Function	Domain	Range
$\sin x$	All real numbers	$-1 \leq \sin x \leq 1$
$\cos x$	All real numbers	$-1 \leq \cos x \leq 1$
$\tan x$	$x \neq \pi/2 + k\pi$	All real numbers
$\sin^{-1} x$	$-1 \leq x \leq 1$	$-\pi/2 \leq \sin^{-1} x \leq \pi/2$
$\cos^{-1} x$	$-1 \leq x \leq 1$	$0 \leq \cos^{-1} x \leq \pi$
$\tan^{-1} x$	All real numbers	$-\pi/2 < \tan^{-1} x < \pi/2$

For greater understanding, the graphs which follow display angles measured in degrees; you will be expected to use radians as well.

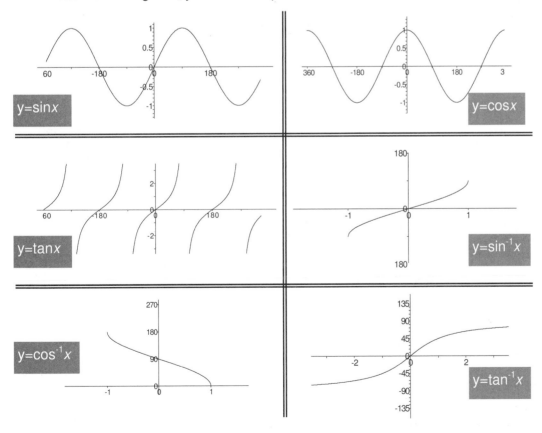

Trigonometric Formulae

You are provided with a whole range of trigonometric formulae which, although available in the exam, are best learnt. Otherwise you may not recognise when to use a particular formula. What do we use them for?

- Simplifying trigonometric expressions
- Solving trigonometric equations
- Helping to integrate and differentiate awkward functions
- Working out *more* trigonometric formulae!

The formulae divide comfortably into groups.

The Pythogorean identities: The first two of these tend to appear more often than the third.

- $\sin^2\theta + \cos^2\theta = 1$
- $1 + \tan^2\theta = \sec^2\theta$
- $1 + \cot^2\theta = \text{cosec}^2\theta$

> Except for linear functions, you must remember that
> $$f(a + b) \neq f(a) + f(b)$$
> although such expressions can often be simplified in other ways. Which of these will simplify?
> $$\sin(a + b)$$
> $$(a + b)^2$$
> $$\sqrt{(a + b)}$$
> $$\ln(a + b)$$
> $$e^{a + b}$$
> *(Answers: 1, 2 and 5)*

The addition formulae: You must never simplify an expression such as $\sin(30° + x)$ as $\sin 30° + \sin x$. The six addition formulae which enable you to remove the brackets are:

- $\sin(A \pm B) = \sin A \cos B \pm \cos A \sin B$
- $\cos(A \pm B) = \cos A \cos B \mp \sin A \sin B$
- $\tan(A \pm B) = \dfrac{\tan A \pm \tan B}{1 \mp \tan A \tan B}$

The double angle formulae: The equation $\sin x = \sin 2x$ cannot be solved directly because it is not possible to work with the x and the $2x$ at the same time. The double angle formulae help us to simplify such expressions. Note that there is only one formula for sin2A, three for cos2A, one for tan2A.

> You are required to *learn* the proofs for the addition formulae and the double angle formulae.

- $\sin 2A = 2\sin A \cos A$
- $\cos 2A = \cos^2 A - \sin^2 A$
  $= 2\cos^2 A - 1$ *(using $\sin^2 A = 1 - \cos^2 A$)*
  $= 1 - 2\sin^2 A$ *(using $\cos^2 A = 1 - \sin^2 A$)*
- $\tan 2A = \dfrac{2\tan A}{1 - \tan^2 A}$

How are the formulae used: Much of the algebra you learn enables you to simplify expressions, or rewrite them in different ways, with the aim of solving equations, differentiating or integrating. The identities listed above extend this idea into trigonometry, and the examples in the next section show how they can be used to help solve trigonometric equations.

YOU SOLVE

Given that $\sin x = \frac{5}{8}$, find an exact value for sin2x.

Combine the formula for sin2x with the little trick shown in the middle of page 34.

$$x = \frac{5\sqrt{39}}{32}$$

🖳 The question above is an ideal case where you should check your answer on the GDC. Find x using $\sin^{-1}x$, then find sin2x. Check this decimal answer is the same as the exact answer.

Solving Trigonometric Equations

The basics: Because all trigonometric functions are periodic there will always be an infinite number of solutions to any trig equation; that is why all questions will restrict the range of solutions – make sure you take note of the given range. In the examples that follow, the solutions are such that $0° \leq x \leq 360°$. If the range is given in radians, your answers must be in radians.

An example of the simplest equations is given on page 36. Suppose you are asked to solve $2\sin 2x + 1 = 0.64$. There will be 4 solutions (because of the $2x$), and the way to find them is:

- Reduce the equation so that the LHS just has the sin function...................... $\sin 2x = -0.18$
- Calculate $\sin^{-1}(-0.18)$...................... $190°$ and $350°$
- Find the next two angles by adding $360°$...................... $550°$ and $710°$
- These will be values of $2x$, so the four solutions for x are .... $95°, 175°, 275°, 355°$

Solutions worked out to the nearest degree

Using the identities: The following examples show how the identities can be used in a variety of situations. In each case, we are aiming to get an equation with just one trig function in it which can then be solved as above. The last part is left for you to complete in each case!

Example 1 – Using an addition formula. Easily recognisable because of the brackets.

$$2\sin\theta = 3\cos(\theta - 60°)$$
$$2\sin\theta = 3\cos\theta\cos 60° + 3\sin\theta\sin 60°$$
$$2\sin\theta = \frac{3}{2}\cos\theta + \frac{3\sqrt{3}}{2}\sin\theta$$
$$4\sin\theta = 3\cos\theta + 3\sqrt{3}\sin\theta$$
$$(4 - 3\sqrt{3})\sin\theta = 3\cos\theta$$
$$\tan\theta = \frac{3}{4 - 3\sqrt{3}} = -2.51$$

Note how we can get a tan function from here. We couldn't if there was an extra numerical term.

Solutions: $\theta = 111.7°$ or $291.7°$

Example 2 – Using the sin2x formula. An equation cannot be solved if it has functions of both x and 2x in it.

$$2\sin 2\theta = 3\sin\theta$$
$$4\sin\theta\cos\theta = 3\sin\theta$$
$$4\sin\theta\cos\theta - 3\sin\theta = 0$$
$$\sin\theta(4\cos\theta - 3) = 0$$
$$\sin\theta = 0 \text{ or } \cos\theta = 0.75$$

Don't divide by $\sin\theta$ - you will lose some solutions. Always factorise.

Solutions: $\theta = 0°, 41.4°, 180°, 318.6°, 360°$

Example 3 – Using the tan2x formula – often a case of "try it and see."

$$\tan\theta\tan 2\theta = 1$$
$$\tan\theta \times \frac{2\tan\theta}{1 - \tan^2\theta} = 1$$
$$2\tan^2\theta = 1 - \tan^2\theta$$
$$\tan^2\theta = \frac{1}{3}$$
$$\tan\theta = \pm\sqrt{\frac{1}{3}}$$

Multiply both sides by $1 - \tan^2\theta$

This will give 4 solutions

Solutions: $\theta = 30°, 150°, 210°, 330°$

Example 4 – Using the cos2x formulae – often this leads to a quadratic equation.

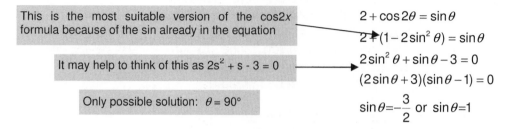

This is the most suitable version of the cos2x formula because of the sin already in the equation

It may help to think of this as $2s^2 + s - 3 = 0$

Only possible solution: $\theta = 90°$

$$2 + \cos 2\theta = \sin\theta$$
$$2 + (1 - 2\sin^2\theta) = \sin\theta$$
$$2\sin^2\theta + \sin\theta - 3 = 0$$
$$(2\sin\theta + 3)(\sin\theta - 1) = 0$$
$$\sin\theta = -\frac{3}{2} \text{ or } \sin\theta = 1$$

If you can, and if you have time, always substitute at least one of your answers into the original equation. If you find it doesn't work, first check that you have copied the question correctly, then check through the working carefully, paying particular attention to minus signs.

YOU SOLVE

By using one of the double angle formulae, find all the solutions of cos2θ = 2sin$^2\theta$ in the interval [0, π]. *Note that you must use the double angle formula to answer the question, so you cannot solve this equation on your GDC.*

$$\theta = \frac{\pi}{6} \text{ or } \frac{5\pi}{6}$$

YOU SOLVE

Solve sec^2x = 8cos$x$ for -180º ≤ x ≤ 180º, showing all your working.
There is no point using 1 + tan^2x since you will still have 2 different trigonometric functions. What else can you do with secx?

x = -60º or 60º

YOU SOLVE

Solve 3sin$x$ = tan$x$, given that 0 ≤ x ≤ π.
Use the formula for tanx, get rid of the bottom line, then everything over to the left hand side and then factorise.

x = 0, 1.23, π

The Solution of Triangles

Sine and Cosine Rules: Right angled triangles can be solved by the familiar methods of "SOHCAHTOA" trigonometry and Pythagoras' Theorem. For triangles which are *not* right-angled we use the sine and cosine rules. The triangle on the right has the conventional notation of small letters for the lengths of sides and capital letters for the angles opposite. To find lengths and angles, use:

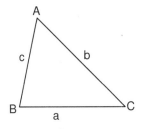

- The sine rule if 2 sides and 2 angles are involved
- The cosine rule if 3 sides and 1 angle are involved

SINE RULE	COSINE RULE
$\dfrac{a}{\sin A} = \dfrac{b}{\sin B} = \dfrac{c}{\sin C}$	$c^2 = a^2 + b^2 - 2ab\cos C$ *(for a side)* $\cos C = \dfrac{a^2 + b^2 - c^2}{2ab}$ *(for an angle)*

> When using the sine rule to find an *angle* there can be *two* answers when you take the $\sin^{-1}$, one acute and one obtuse. Look at the context to decide which answer you want.

Don't be put off by the letters. Basically, the sine rule says the ratio of side/sine is the same for each pair of sides and angles. And in the cosine rule, ensure that the side on the LHS of the equation matches the angle on the RHS.

In triangle PQR, angle P = 30°, PQ = 5 cm and QR = 4cm. Find the possible lengths of PR.

The diagram shows how two lengths are possible. First we must find θ.

$\dfrac{\sin\theta}{5} = \dfrac{\sin 30}{4} \Rightarrow \sin\theta = \dfrac{5}{8} \Rightarrow \theta = 38.7°$ or $141.3°$

(*Both these solutions are valid because neither brings the angle total over 180°*)

Now use the sine rule again (twice) to find the lengths of PR. First, we need angle Q: this is 111.3° or 8.7°.

$\dfrac{PR}{\sin 111.3} = \dfrac{4}{\sin 30}$ or $\dfrac{PR}{\sin 8.7} = \dfrac{4}{\sin 30}$ giving **PR = 7.45cm or 1.21cm**

(*We could have used the cosine rule in the last part, but if you <u>can</u> use the sine rule, it's quicker*)

YOU SOLVE

A cuboid has dimensions as shown in the diagram. Find the angle PWR to the nearest tenth of a degree. *(Find the lengths PW, WR and RP – keeping the square roots – draw the triangle PWR, use the cosine rule)*

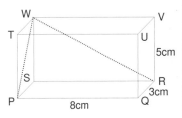

Angle PWR = 63.0°

Area of a non-right angled triangle: If you know two sides of a triangle, and the size of the angle between the two sides, then the area of the triangle can be found using:

- Area $= \dfrac{1}{2}ab\sin C$

The diagram shows a triangle with sides 5, 7 and 8. Find the size of the smallest angle and the area of the triangle.

The smallest angle is opposite the smallest side, 5.

$\cos x = \dfrac{7^2 + 8^2 - 5^2}{2 \times 7 \times 8} = 0.786$. So the angle is **38.2°**

Area $= \frac{1}{2} \times 7 \times 8 \times \sin 38.2° =$ **17.3**

(Remember that the angle used in the area formula must be between the two sides used).

Graphing Periodic Functions

The connection between functions and transformations is covered on page 23. The functions $a\sin b(x + c) + d$ and $a\cos b(x + c) + d$ are a little special because each of the constants a, b, c and d have specific meanings which relate to "real-life" functions. The examples below use degrees for greater understanding, but most of the exam questions will use radians.

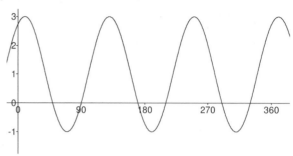

$$y = 2\sin 3(x + 20°) + 1$$

- The 20 translates the graph $-20°$ horizontally.
- The 3 makes the graph cycle 3 times faster than $y = \sin x$, ie the period is 120° rather than 360°. The *frequency* is therefore multiplied by 3.

The period is calculated as
$$\frac{360}{b} \text{ or } \frac{2\pi}{b}$$

- The 2 multiplies the *amplitude* by 2, ie the range of y is -2 to 2 rather than -1 to 1.
- The 1 translates the graph vertically, so the range of y become -1 to 3.

Sketching a graph such as this can also help us to see where solutions to equations of the form $a\sin(bx + c) + d = 0$ are going to occur.

A wave of water passing a fixed point is modelled by the function $h = 0.5\cos(0.25\pi t)$ where h is the height of the water (in metres) above the point and t is the time (in seconds).
i)   **What is the period of the wave?**
ii)   **Draw a sketch of the function for $0 \leq t \leq 16$.**
iii)   **Find the times for $0 \leq t \leq 16$ for which the wave height is 0.35m.**

i)   The period of the wave is $\dfrac{2\pi}{0.25\pi} = \underline{\textbf{8s}}$

ii)   The amplitude will be 0.5m, the period is 8s, and the graph is based on $\cos x$.

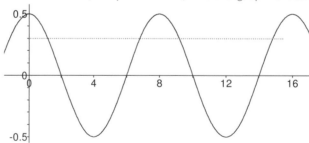

iii)   The dotted line on the graph shows that there are 4 solutions between 0 and 16.

$$0.5\cos 0.25\pi t = 0.35$$

$$\cos 0.25\pi t = 0.7$$

$$0.25\pi t = 0.795, 5.488, 7.078, 11.77$$

So $\underline{t = \textbf{1.01s, 6.99s, 9.01s, 15.0s}}$

(NB: The solutions in line 3 are calculated by first finding $\cos^{-1}0.7$; this gives 0.795; the second solution is 2π - 0.795; the other two are found by adding 2π to the first two).

MATRICES

Basics of Matrices

A matrix is essentially a table of numbers enclosed in brackets. Most of the matrices you meet will be "square" – they have the same numbers of rows and columns. The numbers in a matrix are called the *elements* of the matrix, and the *order* of a matrix is the number of rows and columns it has. Thus a 2×3 matrix has 2 rows and 3 columns.

▤ It is essential that you are familiar with the matrix features of your GDC. Make sure you can do each of the following:
- Enter and edit matrices of any size
- Find the determinant of a matrix
- Find the inverse of a matrix
- Perform matrix calculations

However, since a question may be asked where some of the elements of a matrix are algebraic, you must also be able to carry out matrix operations without a calculator.

Algebra of matrices: Matrices are usually denoted by capital letters.
- If **A** = **B** then all the corresponding elements of the two matrices are the same.
- Matrices can be added or subtracted by adding or subtracting corresponding elements. For example,

$$\begin{pmatrix} 2 & 4 \\ 0 & -1 \end{pmatrix} + \begin{pmatrix} 3 & -4 \\ 2 & 2 \end{pmatrix} = \begin{pmatrix} 5 & 0 \\ 2 & 1 \end{pmatrix}$$

- Multiplying by a scalar will multiply each element by the scalar. eg: If $\mathbf{A} = \begin{pmatrix} 2 & 1 \\ -3 & 4 \end{pmatrix}$ then $2\mathbf{A} = \begin{pmatrix} 4 & 2 \\ -6 & 8 \end{pmatrix}$

- Multiplication of matrices is a rather curious operation. To multiply two matrices, split the first into rows, the second into columns. Then continue like this:

> Important: unlike ordinary algebra, **AB** ≠ **BA** in general.

$$\left(\begin{array}{c|c} a & b \\ \hline c & d \end{array} \right) \left(\begin{array}{c|c} p & q \\ r & s \end{array} \right) = \begin{pmatrix} ap + br & aq + bs \\ cp + dr & cq + ds \end{pmatrix}$$

Note that the answer to 1st row × 1st column goes in the R_1C_1 position in the answer matrix, and so on.

It is possible to multiply non-square matrices, but only if the number of columns in the first is equal to the number of rows in the second. eg:

$$\begin{pmatrix} 2 & 0 & -2 \\ 3 & 1 & 2 \end{pmatrix} \left(\begin{array}{c|c} 1 & -1 \\ 4 & 2 \\ 0 & 2 \end{array} \right) = \begin{pmatrix} 2 & -6 \\ 7 & 3 \end{pmatrix}$$ (The lines

have only been included in an attempt to be helpful).

> Note that we are multiplying a (3×2) by a (2×3). The inner numbers show that the multiplication is possible, the outer ones give the size of the answer matrix.

The identity matrix: When multiplying numbers, 1 is called the *identity* because $a \times 1 = 1 \times a = a$; that is, it leaves other numbers unchanged. For multiplication, the 2×2 identity matrix is

$\begin{pmatrix} 1 & 0 \\ 0 & 1 \end{pmatrix}$ and the 3×3 is $\begin{pmatrix} 1 & 0 & 0 \\ 0 & 1 & 0 \\ 0 & 0 & 1 \end{pmatrix}$. The identity matrix is denoted using **I**. So for any matrix **A**, **AI** = **IA** = **A**.

> Here is the identity matrix in action:
> $$\begin{pmatrix} 2 & 1 \\ 4 & 3 \end{pmatrix} \begin{pmatrix} 1 & 0 \\ 0 & 1 \end{pmatrix} = \begin{pmatrix} 2 & 1 \\ 4 & 3 \end{pmatrix}$$

Zero matrices: In a zero matrix every element is 0. Zero matrices are rather dull!

Determinants and Inverse Matrices

Determinants: The determinant of a square matrix is a rather useful number associated with it. You need to be able to calculate the determinant of both 2×2 and 3×3 matrices.

The 2×2 case is easy. If $\mathbf{M} = \begin{pmatrix} a & b \\ c & d \end{pmatrix}$ then $\det\mathbf{M} = ad - bc$.

Note the result that if you multiply two matrices $\mathbf{A}$ and $\mathbf{B}$ together, $\det\mathbf{AB} = \det\mathbf{A}\det\mathbf{B}$.

For a 3×3 it works like this:

$$\det\begin{pmatrix} a & b & c \\ d & e & f \\ g & h & i \end{pmatrix} = a(ei - fh) - b(di - fg) + c(dh - eg).$$ This is rather dry to remember. Another way is more pictorial: take element a, cross out the row and column it is in, and then multiply by the determinant of the matrix formed by the remaining elements – like this: $\begin{pmatrix} a & \cancel{b} & \cancel{c} \\ \cancel{d} & e & f \\ \cancel{g} & h & i \end{pmatrix}$. Now do the same for b (but *subtract* the number you get), and then finally for c (this time adding again). Verify that you can work out the determinant of $\begin{pmatrix} 2 & 1 & 3 \\ -1 & 4 & 0 \\ 1 & 2 & -2 \end{pmatrix}$ as -36.

Inverse of square matrix: Using numbers as an example again, the inverse of 4, say, is $\frac{1}{4}$ because $4 \times \frac{1}{4} = 1$, the identity. So the inverse of matrix $\mathbf{A}$ has to be found such that $\mathbf{AA^{-1}} = \mathbf{I}$. For a 2×2 matrix $\begin{pmatrix} a & b \\ c & d \end{pmatrix}$, the procedure is:

- Work out the determinant
- Swap round a and d
- Change the signs of b and c
- Divide by the determinant (either by dividing each element or by putting a fraction in front of the matrix).

Thus, the inverse of $\begin{pmatrix} 2 & 3 \\ 1 & 4 \end{pmatrix}$ is $\frac{1}{5}\begin{pmatrix} 4 & -3 \\ -1 & 2 \end{pmatrix} = \begin{pmatrix} 0.8 & -0.6 \\ -0.2 & 0.4 \end{pmatrix}$.

Since the inverse of a 3×3 is much harder to calculate, you will always be able to use your calculator to find it. However, the principle that $\mathbf{AA^{-1}} = \mathbf{I}$ is the same as the following question demonstrates.

$$\mathbf{M} = \begin{pmatrix} 2 & -1 & p \\ 1 & 2 & 0 \\ 2 & 1 & 2 \end{pmatrix}, \ \mathbf{M^{-1}} = \frac{1}{2}\begin{pmatrix} -4 & -6 & 8 \\ 2 & 4 & -4 \\ 3 & q & -5 \end{pmatrix}.$$ Find p and q.

Since $\mathbf{MM^{-1}} = \mathbf{I}$, we can choose to calculate, for example, R1 $\times$ C1 knowing that the result will be 1. So, $2 \times -2 + -1 \times 1 + p \times 1.5 = 1 \Rightarrow -4 - 1 + 1.5p = 1$, giving $\underline{p = 4}$. Note how the fraction in front of $\mathbf{M^{-1}}$ has been included in the calculation.

Choosing R2 $\times$ C2 for the calculation of q would not help because of the zero at the end of R2; try it and see. So we do R3 $\times$ C2, and this will give 0. So, $-6 + 2 + q = 0$, giving $\underline{q = 4}$. 🖩 Enter matrix M into your calculator, and check your answer by calculating M^{-1}.

Solving Equations Using Matrices

Singular matrices: A matrix with a zero determinant is called *singular* and has no inverse. A 2×2 singular matrix always has columns which are multiples of each other eg: $\begin{pmatrix} 4 & 10 \\ 2 & 5 \end{pmatrix}$, but no such simple rule works for a 3×3 – you must put the determinant equal to zero.

Find the value of _k_ which for which the matrix $\begin{pmatrix} 2 & 4 & 1 \\ k & k & -1 \\ 5 & 7 & -2 \end{pmatrix}$ **is singular.**

Find the determinant in terms of k and put equal to 0.

YOU SOLVE

$\underline{k = 1}$

Solving 2×2 equations: Consider the pair of simultaneous equations shown on the right. We can rewrite them in a matrix form like this: $\begin{pmatrix} 2 & -1 \\ 3 & 4 \end{pmatrix}\begin{pmatrix} x \\ y \end{pmatrix} = \begin{pmatrix} 5 \\ 9 \end{pmatrix}$. Using matrix algebra, the form of the equation is **MX = A**, where **X** is the matrix we want to find. Matrix division is not possible, but we can remove the **M** from the LHS by multiplying by its inverse.

$\begin{cases} 2x - y = 5 \\ 3x + 4y = 9 \end{cases}$

$\quad$ **MX = A**
$\quad$ **M⁻¹MX = M⁻¹A**
$\quad$ **X = M⁻¹A**

So the solution is found by pre-multiplying **A** by **M⁻¹**.

Note that we multiply *in front* on both sides – you could not pre-multiply on the LHS then post-multiply on the RHS.

$$\begin{pmatrix} x \\ y \end{pmatrix} = \tfrac{1}{11}\begin{pmatrix} 4 & 1 \\ -3 & 2 \end{pmatrix}\begin{pmatrix} 5 \\ 9 \end{pmatrix} = \tfrac{1}{11}\begin{pmatrix} 29 \\ 3 \end{pmatrix}$$

So, $x = \frac{29}{11}$, $y = \frac{3}{11}$ and, as with any sort of equation, you can check your answers by resubstituting the values in the original equation.

🖩 The equation can also be solved on the calculator: first, enter $\mathbf{A} = \begin{pmatrix} 2 & -1 \\ 3 & 4 \end{pmatrix}$ $\mathbf{B} = \begin{pmatrix} 5 \\ 9 \end{pmatrix}$, then find the solution by calculating **A⁻¹B**.

Solving 3×3 equations: Using the calculator method shown above, find the solutions to the simultaneous equations:

$$\begin{cases} 2x + 4y - z = 12 \\ x - y + 4z = 6 \\ 4x + 5y - z = 17 \end{cases}$$

(Your solution should be x = 1, y = 3, z = 2)

An alternative method (and one which you need to know) is to use *row reduction* (also called *Gaussian elimination*). The aim is to perform numerical operations on the rows of matrix **M** so that you create three zeroes in the bottom left hand corner, carrying out the same operations of matrix **A** at the same time. This renders three new equations which are very simple to solve.

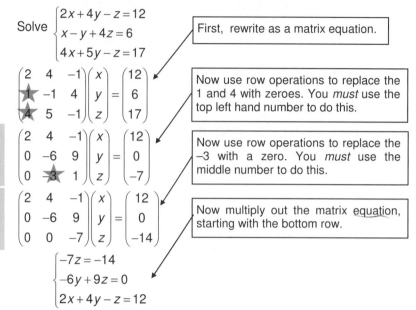

Solve $\begin{cases} 2x + 4y - z = 12 \\ x - y + 4z = 6 \\ 4x + 5y - z = 17 \end{cases}$

First, rewrite as a matrix equation.

$$\begin{pmatrix} 2 & 4 & -1 \\ 1 & -1 & 4 \\ 4 & 5 & -1 \end{pmatrix} \begin{pmatrix} x \\ y \\ z \end{pmatrix} = \begin{pmatrix} 12 \\ 6 \\ 17 \end{pmatrix}$$

Now use row operations to replace the 1 and 4 with zeroes. You *must* use the top left hand number to do this.

Leave R1 unchanged
R2 becomes 2 × R2 − R1
R3 becomes R3 − 2 × R1

$$\begin{pmatrix} 2 & 4 & -1 \\ 0 & -6 & 9 \\ 0 & -3 & 1 \end{pmatrix} \begin{pmatrix} x \\ y \\ z \end{pmatrix} = \begin{pmatrix} 12 \\ 0 \\ -7 \end{pmatrix}$$

Now use row operations to replace the −3 with a zero. You *must* use the middle number to do this.

Leave R1 unchanged
Leave R2 unchanged
R3 becomes 2 × R3 − R2

$$\begin{pmatrix} 2 & 4 & -1 \\ 0 & -6 & 9 \\ 0 & 0 & -7 \end{pmatrix} \begin{pmatrix} x \\ y \\ z \end{pmatrix} = \begin{pmatrix} 12 \\ 0 \\ -14 \end{pmatrix}$$

Now multiply out the matrix equation, starting with the bottom row.

$$\begin{cases} -7z = -14 \\ -6y + 9z = 0 \\ 2x + 4y - z = 12 \end{cases}$$

...which can be solved easily. The first gives $z = 2$. Substituting this value into the second gives $y = 3$. And substituting both into the third gives $x = 1$.

Clearly, it is much faster to use a calculator. But as soon as letters replace numbers, you must use row operations.

Equations with non-unique solutions: What happens when you try to solve simultaneous equations using a matrix which turns out to be singular? There can be no inverse matrix, because finding the inverse involves dividing by the determinant.

2 × 2 equations: If you consider the two equations as lines, then they will always intersect *unless* they are parallel (or the same line). And it is easy to tell if they are parallel because the LHS of the two equations will be multiples of each other. The possibilities are:

Non-singular matrix	1 solution	Solution represents the point of intersection of lines
Singular matrix	0 solutions	Parallel lines
	∞ solutions	Coincident lines

3 × 3 equations: Now we consider the equations as planes, and the possible configurations are more complex. Again, parallel planes are easy to identify because they have left hand sides which are the same or multiples of each other.

Non-singular matrix	1 solution	Solution represents the point which is the intersection of 3 planes
Singular matrix	0 solutions	All 3 planes parallel
		2 planes parallel
		3 planes with a common axis – a *prism*
	∞ solutions	3 planes meet along a common line – a *sheaf*

How can we tell if the matrix is singular, (besides finding the determinant with a calculator)? When carrying out row operations, you will find one of the rows reduces to three zeroes. If the right hand matrix also has a 0 in the same row, there will be ∞ solutions; if it is not 0, then there are no solutions.

...because $0x + 0y + 0z = 0$ has ∞ solutions whereas $0x + 0y + 0z = k$ has none.

Find the values of a and b such that the matrix equation $\begin{pmatrix} 1 & 1 & -4 \\ 5 & 2 & -9 \\ 4 & -2 & a \end{pmatrix} \begin{pmatrix} x \\ y \\ z \end{pmatrix} = \begin{pmatrix} 1 \\ 7 \\ b \end{pmatrix}$ has an

infinite number of solutions.

Performing row operations (fill in the boxes to say what they are)

$$\begin{pmatrix} 1 & 1 & -4 \\ 0 & -3 & 11 \\ 0 & -6 & a+16 \end{pmatrix} \begin{pmatrix} x \\ y \\ z \end{pmatrix} = \begin{pmatrix} 1 \\ 2 \\ b-4 \end{pmatrix}$$

☐

☐

$$\begin{pmatrix} 1 & 1 & -4 \\ 0 & -3 & 11 \\ 0 & 0 & a-6 \end{pmatrix} \begin{pmatrix} x \\ y \\ z \end{pmatrix} = \begin{pmatrix} 1 \\ 2 \\ b-8 \end{pmatrix}$$

☐

Thus, for infinite solutions, $a = 6$, $b = 8$

The following system of equations has an infinite number of solutions.

$$\begin{cases} 2x-y-9z=7 \\ x+2y+3z=1 \\ 2x+y-3z=p \end{cases}$$

Find the value of p.

YOU SOLVE

$p = 5$

---

a) **Find the values of k for which the system of equations** $\begin{cases} kx+z=1 \\ 3x-y+kz=1 \\ 5x+3y+z=1 \end{cases}$ **has no solution.**

b) **Find the solution of the equations when $k = 3$.**

YOU SOLVE

a) $k = 2$ or $8/3$ (b) $x = 0.375$, $y = -0.25$, $z = -0.125$

VECTORS

Basics of Vectors

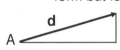

A vector

Same length, different direction – so different vector

Notation: Think of a vector as representing a movement, or displacement, in a plane. This can be represented by an arrow. The vector can be defined in several ways:

- Using a single small letter. Bold type in printed text, line underneath or arrow on top in handwriting.
- Using the named points at either end, arrow on top.
- Using a "column vector" to show the displacement in the x, y and z (if applicable) directions.
- In the form $a\boldsymbol{i} + b\boldsymbol{j}$ where $\boldsymbol{i}$ and $\boldsymbol{j}$ are unit vectors in the x and y directions (this is equivalent to the column vector form but less easy to use).

This vector could be written as:

$$\overrightarrow{AB}, \boldsymbol{d}, \begin{pmatrix} 6 \\ 3 \end{pmatrix}, 6\boldsymbol{i} + 3\boldsymbol{j} \text{ (as examples)}$$

The column vector form is useful because we can work out the length and direction of the vector using Pythagoras and arctan (or using appropriate calculator functions).

Position and displacement vectors: If a vector is used to define the position of a point then it is known as a *position vector*. It will always start at the origin. The components of the column vector will always be the same as the coordinates of the point. *Displacement* vectors differ from position vectors in that they have no specific position – they just represent a *change* in position.

Operating with vectors: If you move along a vector $\boldsymbol{a}$ then along a vector $\boldsymbol{b}$, the single displacement which takes you to the end position is defined as vector $\boldsymbol{a} + \boldsymbol{b}$. The length of $\boldsymbol{a} + \boldsymbol{b}$ is *not* the length of $\boldsymbol{a}$ plus the length of $\boldsymbol{b}$; it is shorter. However, if $\boldsymbol{a}$ and $\boldsymbol{b}$ are written as column vectors, then adding them will give vector

$\boldsymbol{a} + \boldsymbol{b}$. For example: $\begin{pmatrix} 6 \\ -2 \end{pmatrix} + \begin{pmatrix} -4 \\ 5 \end{pmatrix} = \begin{pmatrix} 2 \\ 3 \end{pmatrix}$.

A vector can be *multiplied* by a number. For example, $2\boldsymbol{a}$ has the same direction as $\boldsymbol{a}$ but is twice as long. Using column vectors, eg:

$2\begin{pmatrix} 3 \\ 5 \end{pmatrix} = \begin{pmatrix} 6 \\ 10 \end{pmatrix}$. And a *minus* sign reverses the direction of a vector.

YOU SOLVE

A quadrilateral OABC has points O(0, 0) and A(4, 1).

i) If AB = $\begin{pmatrix} 1 \\ -2.5 \end{pmatrix}$, find the coordinates of B.

ii) OC is $\begin{pmatrix} -1 \\ k \end{pmatrix}$. Find k such that CB is parallel to OA. What is the ratio of lengths of OA to CB?

<u>B = (5, -1.5)</u>,   <u>k = -3</u>,   <u>1:1.5</u>

Vector subtraction: To get from A to B using vectors, the path is

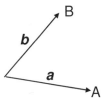

$-a + b$ or $b - a$. Thus the vector $\overrightarrow{AB} = b - a$. This general principle should be remembered. It also works with position vectors. For example, if A is (4, 3) and B is (6, -1) then A and B have position vectors $\begin{pmatrix} 4 \\ 3 \end{pmatrix}$ and $\begin{pmatrix} 6 \\ -1 \end{pmatrix}$. So

vector $\overrightarrow{AB} = b - a = \begin{pmatrix} 6 \\ -1 \end{pmatrix} - \begin{pmatrix} 4 \\ 3 \end{pmatrix} = \begin{pmatrix} 2 \\ -4 \end{pmatrix}$.

> Alternatively:
> $OA = 4i + 3j$, $OB = 6i - j$
> $AB = OB - OA$
> $= (6i - j) - (4i + 3j)$
> $= (2i - 4j)$

Three Dimensional Vectors: Conventional geometry is harder in three dimensions than in two: using vectors, the routines and calculations are pretty much the same in *any* number of dimensions - even 4! Thus vectors provide us with a powerful framework for solving problems in 3-d geometry.

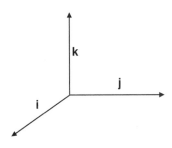

> It is always hard to draw accurate diagrams of 3-d vectors. If it *has* to be done, the configuration shown left is often used, but others are possible.

Magnitude of vectors: The *magnitude* (or length) can be found by using Pythagoras' Theorem in two or three dimensions as appropriate. The length of $2i + 3j - 5k$ is $\sqrt{(2^2 + 3^2 + (-5)^2)} = \sqrt{38}$. Use the modulus sign to represent magnitude. Thus, $|p|$ is the magnitude of p.

---

a) **Show that A(2, 0, 3), B(3, 6, -1) and C(4.5, 15, -7) are collinear.**
b) **Find the ratio of AB:BC**
a) *Prove that **AC** is a multiple of **AB**.*

YOU SOLVE

<u>1.5</u>

Unit vectors: Any vector with length 1 is a *unit vector*. The three vectors *i*, *j* and *k* are unit vectors which form the basis of the 3-d coordinate system. As with 2-d vectors, it is easier to use the

column format eg: $\begin{pmatrix} 2 \\ 3 \\ 4 \end{pmatrix}$ rather than $2i + 3j + 4k$. To find a unit

vector in a particular direction, divide the given vector by its length.

Find the unit vector in the direction $2i - j + 2k$.

The length of the vector is $\sqrt{4+1+4} = 3$.

So the unit vector in the same direction is $\frac{2}{3}i - \frac{1}{3}j + \frac{2}{3}k$.

Scalar (Dot) Product

Definition: The scalar product is a number which can be calculated from two vectors. On its own it has no real significance, but is used particularly in connection with angles between vectors. The scalar product of two vectors (2-d or 3-d) **a** and **b** is defined as: $\mathbf{a.b} = |\mathbf{a}||\mathbf{b}|\cos\theta$ where θ is the angle between the directions of the two vectors. This formula can be read as: "The dot product of vectors **a** and **b** = the length of **a** times the length of **b** times the cosine of the angle between them." If the vectors are defined in column form, an alternative way of calculating the scalar product

is: $\begin{pmatrix} a_1 \\ a_2 \\ a_3 \end{pmatrix} . \begin{pmatrix} b_1 \\ b_2 \\ b_3 \end{pmatrix} = a_1b_1 + a_2b_2 + a_3b_3$.

Properties of the scalar product: Many of the properties are similar to the algebraic multiplication of numbers $a \times b$.

- $\mathbf{a.b} = \mathbf{b.a}$
- $\mathbf{a.(b + c)} = \mathbf{a.b} + \mathbf{a.c}$
- $(m\mathbf{a}).(n\mathbf{b}) = mn(\mathbf{a.b})$

An important property is that perpendicular vectors have a dot product = 0 (since $\cos 90° = 0$)

- If $\mathbf{a} \perp \mathbf{b}$ then $\mathbf{a.b} = 0$ (and vice versa).

Angle between two vectors: The dot product provides a convenient way of calculating the angle between two vectors.

eg: Find the angle between $\mathbf{a} = 2\mathbf{i} + 3\mathbf{j} - \mathbf{k}$ and $\mathbf{b} = 4\mathbf{i} - 2\mathbf{j} + 3\mathbf{k}$. (Remember that this is an alternative form to the column vector).

The length of **a** is $\sqrt{2^2 + 3^2 + (-1)^2} = \sqrt{14}$ and of **b** is $\sqrt{4^2 + (-2)^2 + 3^2} = \sqrt{29}$. So $\mathbf{a.b} = \sqrt{14}\sqrt{29}\cos\theta$. But $\mathbf{a.b}$ can also be calculated using column vectors:

$$\mathbf{a.b} = \begin{pmatrix} 2 \\ 3 \\ -1 \end{pmatrix} . \begin{pmatrix} 4 \\ -2 \\ 3 \end{pmatrix} = 8 - 6 - 3 = \text{-1}$$

So, $\sqrt{14}\sqrt{29}\cos\theta = \text{-1}$ and $\cos\theta = \dfrac{-1}{\sqrt{14}\sqrt{29}} = -0.496$. And finally we get the angle θ to be $\cos^{-1}(-0.496) = 92.8°$. If the question asks for the acute angle between the vectors, we must then give the answer $87.2°$.

If $p = 3\mathbf{i} + 2a\mathbf{j} - \mathbf{k}$ and $q = \mathbf{i} + (a-3)\mathbf{j} + (3a-1)\mathbf{k}$, find the values of a such that $p \perp q$.

If they are perpendicular, their dot product will be 0. So, $3 \times 1 + 2a(a-3) + (-1)(3a-1) = 0$. This leads to the quadratic equation $2a^2 - 9a + 4 = 0$, which factorises to $(2a-1)(a-4) = 0$
So, **$a = 0.5$ or 4**

Triangle RST has vertices at R(1, -1, 4), S(2, -1, 0) and T(0, 1, 1).
Find the angle at R and hence the area of the triangle.
Draw a sketch (the actual positions of the points are irrelevant – draw them anywhere, but label them). Use the dot product ($\overrightarrow{RS}.\overrightarrow{RT}$) to find the angle, then use the area formula.

R = 44.5°,   Area = 5.41

Vector (Cross) Product

Definition: Unlike the scalar product, the vector product of two vectors is itself a vector. The cross product is written as $a \times b$ and both a and b have to be 3-d vectors. If the vectors are written in column form, then the cross product is:

$$a \times b = \begin{pmatrix} a_1 \\ a_2 \\ a_3 \end{pmatrix} \times \begin{pmatrix} b_1 \\ b_2 \\ b_3 \end{pmatrix} = \begin{pmatrix} a_2 b_3 - a_3 b_2 \\ a_3 b_1 - a_1 b_3 \\ a_1 b_2 - a_2 b_1 \end{pmatrix} = \begin{vmatrix} \vec{i} & \vec{j} & \vec{k} \\ a_1 & a_2 & a_3 \\ b_1 & b_2 & b_3 \end{vmatrix}$$

Look carefully at the patterns to see how to memorise them.

Applications: The main property of the vector $a \times b$ is that it is perpendicular to both a and b. For example, if $a \times b =$

$$\begin{pmatrix} 2 \\ 1 \\ -3 \end{pmatrix} \times \begin{pmatrix} 0 \\ -2 \\ 4 \end{pmatrix} = \begin{pmatrix} 4-6 \\ 0-8 \\ (-4)-0 \end{pmatrix} = \begin{pmatrix} -2 \\ -8 \\ 4 \end{pmatrix}$$, then $\begin{pmatrix} -2 \\ -8 \\ 4 \end{pmatrix}$ is perpendicular to a

> Use the dot product to test the answer.

and b. This is particularly useful when finding normal vectors to planes.

Another useful property is that $|a \times b| = |a||b|\sin\theta$ where θ is the angle between the two vectors. This expression is equivalent to the area of the parallelogram which can be formed from the two vectors, and also leads to the formula for the area of a triangle formed from the two vectors: Area $= \frac{1}{2}|a \times b|$.

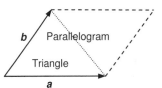

The following is a part of a section B question.

---

i)   **For the vectors $a = 2i + j - 2k$, $b = 2i - j - k$ and $c = i + 2j + 2k$, show that:**
a) $a \times b = -3i - 2j - 4k$
b) $(a \times b) \times c = (-b.c)a$

ii)   **Three points A(2, 1, -2), B(2, -1, -1) and C(1, 2, 2) have position vectors $\overrightarrow{OA}$, $\overrightarrow{OB}$ and $\overrightarrow{OC}$, where O is the origin. These vectors form three concurrent edges of a parallelepiped as shown in the diagram.**
a)   **Find the coordinates of P, Q, R and S.**
b)   **Calculate the volume, V, of the paralleliped, given that**
            $V = |\overrightarrow{OA} \times \overrightarrow{OB}.\overrightarrow{OC}|$

i) Remember that dot product gives a number, cross product gives a vector. Thus, in the last part, you must take the cross product first, otherwise you will be crossing a vector with a number.
ii) The points have an uncanny resemblance to the vectors in part (i). Is this useful??

YOU SOLVE

P(4, 0, -3) Q(3, 3, 0) R(3, 1, 1) S(5, 2, -1);   15

Equations of Lines

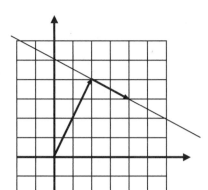

Vector equation of a line: Although we can use the Cartesian equation of a line in 2 dimensions (ie $y = mx + c$), in 3 dimensions it becomes very unwieldy (see below). The *vector equation* of a line is much easier to use, and has the same form in both 2 and 3 dimensions. The line shown in the diagram has a direction given

by the vector $\begin{pmatrix} 2 \\ -1 \end{pmatrix}$. We can find the position vector of any point on

the line by first going along a vector which *takes* us to the line - say, to the point (2, 4) - and then adding any multiple of the direction vector. This gives us the *vector equation* of the line. In

this case it would be: $r = \begin{pmatrix} 2 \\ 4 \end{pmatrix} + t\begin{pmatrix} 2 \\ -1 \end{pmatrix}$.

- The *r* indicates the position vector of a general point on the line and could also be written as $\begin{pmatrix} x \\ y \end{pmatrix}$.

- The vector $\begin{pmatrix} 2 \\ 4 \end{pmatrix}$ is the position of a point on the line – any other point on the line could have been used.

- *t* is called the *parameter.* Different values of *t* give us different points. For example, if $t = 2$, we get the point (6, 2), and every point on the line corresponds to a particular value of *t*.

- The vector $\begin{pmatrix} 2 \\ -1 \end{pmatrix}$ is the *direction vector* of the line. Other multiples, such as $\begin{pmatrix} -4 \\ 2 \end{pmatrix}$ could have been used.

> Any letter can be used for the parameter, including Greek letters. λ is often used.

In general, the vector equation of a line is $r = a + \lambda b$ where *a* is the position vector of a point on the line and *b* is the direction vector. The only difference in 3 dimensions is that *r*, *a* and *b* are 3-d vectors.

Find a vector equation of the line passing through (-3, 4, 1) and (2, -2, 2)

The *direction* vector of the line can be found by subtracting the points (either way round)

This gives: $\begin{pmatrix} -3 \\ 4 \\ 1 \end{pmatrix} - \begin{pmatrix} 2 \\ -2 \\ 2 \end{pmatrix} = \begin{pmatrix} -5 \\ 6 \\ -1 \end{pmatrix}$ Either point can now be used as the *position* vector. The equation

of the line is therefore: $r = \begin{pmatrix} -3 \\ 4 \\ 1 \end{pmatrix} + \lambda \begin{pmatrix} -5 \\ 6 \\ -1 \end{pmatrix}$

Note that in the question above, it also follows that a general point on the line has coordinates $(-3 - 5\lambda, 4 + 6\lambda, 1 - \lambda)$.

Cartesian equation of a line: In 3 dimensions, the general form

is $\dfrac{x - x_0}{l} = \dfrac{y - y_0}{m} = \dfrac{z - z_0}{n}$ where $\begin{pmatrix} l \\ m \\ n \end{pmatrix}$ is the direction vector and

> Suppose the 6 in the direction vector is a 0. The middle fraction is removed from the equation and replaced with $y = 4$, since the y coordinate must now be constant.

(x_0, y_0, z_0) is a point on the line. Since this is the same information as in the vector equation, it is easy to convert from one to the other. The line above therefore has a Cartesian equation $\dfrac{x + 3}{-5} = \dfrac{y - 4}{6} = \dfrac{z - 1}{-1}$ (and each of these fractions equals λ).

Equations of Planes

Vector equation of a plane: The vector equation of a plane is similar to that for a line, except that *two* direction vectors are needed to define a plane. The equation will be of the form $r = a + \lambda b + \mu c$. The problem with this form is that a can be the position vector of *any* point on the plane, and b and c can be any two of the infinite number of directions in the plane. However, it is very easy to find any points on the plane by substituting any values of λ and μ.

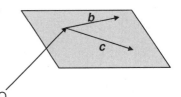

Cartesian equation of a plane: Unlike the line, the Cartesian equation of the plane is much easier to use. It is always of the form $ax + by + cz = d$. Although a plane contains an infinite number of direction vectors, only *one* direction can be perpendicular to a plane. A vector in this direction is called a *normal vector*, and it turns out that the plane $ax + by + cz = d$ has a normal vector $\begin{pmatrix} a \\ b \\ c \end{pmatrix}$.

> Thus, planes with the same left hand side must have the same normal vector, and are therefore parallel to each other. The larger d is, the further away the plane is from the origin.

The vector product gives us a useful way to find the Cartesian equation of a plane given three points in the plane.
- Use the three points to find two direction vectors
- Use the cross product to find a vector perpendicular to these – this will be the normal vector for the plane.
- Write down the LHS of the equation.
- Substitute any of the three points to work out the RHS.

Find the equation of the plane containing points A(2, 4, 0), B(-1, 0, 5) and C(4, 2, -2).

Trying to end up with as many positive values as possible, I choose to find directions **BA** and **CA**.

These are $\begin{pmatrix} 3 \\ 4 \\ -5 \end{pmatrix}$ and $\begin{pmatrix} -2 \\ 2 \\ 2 \end{pmatrix}$. The cross product of these is $\begin{pmatrix} 18 \\ 4 \\ 14 \end{pmatrix}$ which can be simplified (since it is a direction vector) to $\begin{pmatrix} 9 \\ 2 \\ 7 \end{pmatrix}$. Thus the equation begins $9x + 2y + 7z = ...$ By substituting any of the three points, we get $\underline{9x + 2y + 7z = 26.}$ *(Check the other two points satisfy this equation).*

Alternative form for the Cartesian equation: The general form of the equation $ax + by + cz = d$ can be written using the dot product as $\begin{pmatrix} x \\ y \\ z \end{pmatrix} . \begin{pmatrix} a \\ b \\ c \end{pmatrix} = d$ or $r.n = d$, where n is a normal vector. It can also be shown that $d = a.n$ where a is a fixed point on the plane. Thus we get the alternative form $r.n = a.n$ which *looks* like a vector equation but is in fact an alternative expression for the Cartesian equation.

YOU SOLVE

Show that the line $r = \begin{pmatrix} 2 \\ 1 \\ 3 \end{pmatrix} + \lambda \begin{pmatrix} 4 \\ 3 \\ 1 \end{pmatrix}$ is parallel to the plane $x - 2y + 2z = 5$.

Hint: if the line is parallel to the plane, the normal vector to the plane should also be perpendicular to line. Show this with the dot product.

Equations of Lines and Planes – Summary

	Line	Plane
Cartesian Equation	$\dfrac{x-a}{l} = \dfrac{y-b}{m} = \dfrac{z-c}{n}$	$ax + by + cz = d$
Notes	Not as easy to use as the vector equation of a 3d line; convert if necessary.	$\begin{pmatrix} a \\ b \\ c \end{pmatrix}$ is the normal vector.
Vector Equation	$r = \begin{pmatrix} a \\ b \\ c \end{pmatrix} + \lambda \begin{pmatrix} l \\ m \\ n \end{pmatrix}$	$r = \begin{pmatrix} f \\ g \\ h \end{pmatrix} + \lambda \begin{pmatrix} l \\ m \\ n \end{pmatrix} + \mu \begin{pmatrix} p \\ q \\ r \end{pmatrix}$
Notes	The a, b, c, l, m, n are the same as in the Cartesian equation.	Two direction vectors are required to define the plane. The vector equation is less useful than the Cartesian equation.

Find an equation of the plane containing the two lines:

$$\frac{x-1}{3} = \frac{1-y}{4} = z-1 \text{ and } \frac{x+1}{3} = \frac{y-2}{1} = \frac{2-z}{4}.$$

There are lots of points to note here. First, look at the equations:

1. The $z-1$ has no bottom line, so put it over 1.
2. Some of the top lines have been reversed – this is to simplify the fraction when the bottom line is in fact negative.
3. The question does not specify whether to write a Cartesian equation or a vector equation. Because the plane contains the lines, we know points on the plane and we know directions in the plane. So the *vector* equation will be easier to write down.

First, let's rewrite the equations of the lines in a more consistent form.

$$\frac{x-1}{3} = \frac{y-1}{-4} = \frac{z-1}{1} \text{ and } \frac{x+1}{3} = \frac{y-2}{1} = \frac{z-2}{-4}$$

So one of the points on the plane must be (1, 1, 1) (since it lies on the first line); and the two directions of the lines are also two directions of the plane. So the vector equation of the plane is:

$$r = \begin{pmatrix} 1 \\ 1 \\ 1 \end{pmatrix} + \lambda \begin{pmatrix} 3 \\ -4 \\ 1 \end{pmatrix} + \mu \begin{pmatrix} 3 \\ 1 \\ -4 \end{pmatrix}$$

YOU SOLVE

The plane $4x + y - 3z = 6$ contains the line $x - 1 = \dfrac{y-5}{2} = \dfrac{z-1}{k}$. Find the value of k.

Hint: The normal vector to a plane is perpendicular to all directions in the plane

$\underline{k = 2}$

Intersections

You must learn a "library" of techniques which will help you to answer the majority of vector geometry questions. The first group involve intersections between lines and lines, lines and planes, and planes and planes. Throughout, we are working in 3 dimensions.

Intersection of two lines: There are three possible orientations of two lines:

- The two lines intersect
- The two lines are parallel
- The two lines are not parallel and do not intersect (*skew* lines).

We can easily recognise two parallel lines – they have the same direction vector (or they are multiples of each other). In all other cases, we begin by putting the vector equations equal to each other (if a line has a Cartesian equation, convert it).

Find if lines $r = -i + 4j + \lambda(3i - 2j + k)$ and $\dfrac{x-4}{2} = \dfrac{4-y}{3} = \dfrac{z+1}{2}$ meet. If they do, find the point of intersection.

Stage 1: Write the two lines in "condensed parametric" form (my term).

$$\text{Line 1 is } r = \begin{pmatrix} -1+3\lambda \\ 4-2\lambda \\ \lambda \end{pmatrix} \qquad \text{Line 2 is } r = \begin{pmatrix} 4+2\mu \\ 4-3\mu \\ -1+2\mu \end{pmatrix}$$

Make sure you understand how both lines have been converted to this form.

Stage 2: Put the two equations equal to each other to find where they have the same *x, y* and *z* coordinates.

$$-1 + 3\lambda = 4 + 2\mu$$
$$4 - 2\lambda = 4 - 3\mu$$
$$\lambda = -1 + 2\mu$$

Three equations in two unknowns? Two of the equations will be enough to find λ and μ; then, if those values <u>do not</u> satisfy the third equation, the lines do not intersect. Let's try it….

Stage 3: Solve two of the equations (whichever look easiest). Solving the second and third simultaneously gives $\mu = 2$, $\lambda = 3$. Now try these in the first equation: LHS = $-1 + 3 \times 3 = 8$. RHS = $4 + 2 \times 2 = 8$. So the lines *do* intersect.

It is only necessary to sub. one of the values, but do it with both and you have a good check for your answer.

Stage 4: To find the point of intersection, simply substitute λ or μ into the equations of the lines. We get (8, -2, 3) as the point of intersection.

Intersection of a line and a plane: Write the line in "condensed parametric" form and substitute the three components into the equation of the plane. This gives an equation for λ, the solution of which can be used to find the point.

Find where the plane $2x + 3y + z = 7$ and line $r = \begin{pmatrix} 2 \\ -1 \\ -2 \end{pmatrix} + \lambda \begin{pmatrix} 1 \\ 0 \\ 2 \end{pmatrix}$ meet.

If we ended up with $0\lambda = k$, there are no solutions – so the line is parallel to the plane. If we ended up with $0\lambda = 0$, there are ∞ solutions, so the line lies in the plane.

Substituting $x = 2 + \lambda$, $y = -1$ and $z = -2 + 2\lambda$ into the equation of the plane gives: $2(2 + \lambda) + 3(-1) + (-2 + 2\lambda) = 7$, which solves to give $\lambda = 2$. Put this back into the equation of the line to get the point of intersection as (4, -1, 2).

Intersection of two planes: Two planes are either parallel (in which case they have the same or parallel normal vectors) or they intersect along a line. How do we find the equation of the line of intersection? The steps are:

- Use both equations to eliminate one letter, say z.
- Do the same again to eliminate another letter, say y.
- Make the third letter (x) the subject of both equations.
- The Cartesian equation of the line can now be written down.

Find the equation of the line of intersection of the planes:
   $x - y + 2z = 3$ **and** $2x + y + 3z = 1.$

Eliminating y from the equations gives $3x + 5z = 4$.
Eliminating x from the equations gives $3y - z = -5$.

Make z the subject of both to get $z = \dfrac{-3x+4}{5}$ and $z = 3y + 5$

So the equation of the line of intersection is

$$\frac{-3x+4}{5} = 3y + 5 = z \quad \text{or} \quad \frac{x - \frac{4}{3}}{-\frac{5}{3}} = \frac{y + \frac{5}{3}}{\frac{1}{3}} = \frac{z - 0}{1}$$

One way to check this is to see if the point on the line ie $\left(\frac{4}{3}, -\frac{5}{3}, 0\right)$ lies on both planes.

> Although the vector equation of a line is easier to use, this method leads straight to the Cartesian equation. No particular form was specified in the question.

YOU SOLVE

Find the equation of the line of intersection of planes $4x - y - z = 2$ and $3x - y - 2z = -1$

$$x = \frac{y+5}{5} = \frac{z-3}{-1}$$

YOU SOLVE

Find the point where the line $x = 4 + 2t$, $y = -2 - t$, $z = 2 + 3t$ intersects the plane $4x - 3y - z = 4$.

$(0, 0, -4)$

Intersection of three planes: Use the row reduction or inverse matrix techniques discussed on pages 45 – 47. Consider the intersections of the following planes:

$$\begin{cases} x + y + z = 5 \\ 3x - y + 2z = 11 \\ 5x + ay + bz = q \end{cases}$$

Show that when: $a = -3$, $b = 3$, $q = 17$, the planes make a sheaf;
$a = -3$, $b = 3$, $q = 16$, the planes make a prism;
$a = 5$, $b = 5$, $q = 25$, two planes are parallel;
$a = -3$, $b = 2$, $q = 17$, the planes meet at the point $(4, 1, 0)$.

Angles in Three Dimensions

Page 50 shows you how to find the angle between two vectors using the dot product. When dealing with vectors, you will use this technique whenever you need to find an angle. It is then only necessary to decide which two vectors to use.

Angle between two lines: Find the angle between the two line directions.   Lines $r = \begin{pmatrix} 1 \\ -1 \\ 3 \end{pmatrix} + \lambda \begin{pmatrix} 2 \\ 1 \\ 4 \end{pmatrix}$ and $r = \begin{pmatrix} 0 \\ 4 \\ 1 \end{pmatrix} + \lambda \begin{pmatrix} -1 \\ 2 \\ 1 \end{pmatrix}$ have

direction vectors $\begin{pmatrix} 2 \\ 1 \\ 4 \end{pmatrix}$ and $\begin{pmatrix} -1 \\ 2 \\ 1 \end{pmatrix}$. The dot product method gives the angle between these directions, and hence between the lines, as 69.1°.

Angle between a line and a plane: A plane has no single direction, but we can find the angle between the *normal* vector (which has a unique direction) and the direction of the line. Subtracting this from 90° gives the angle between the line and the plane.

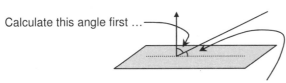

Calculate this angle first ...

...and subtract from 90° to get this one.

Angle between two planes: The angle between two planes is the same as the angle between their normal vectors.

P_1 is the plane $2x - y + 3z = 8$; P_2 is the plane $4x - 2y = 10$. Points R and S have coordinates (4, -1, 4) and (3, 2, 0) respectively.
i)   Find the equation of the plane P_3 which contains point R and is perpendicular to both planes P_1 and P_2.

If a plane is perpendicular to two other planes, its normal vector is perpendicular to their normals (this is very hard to draw, but try it with some books). Thus we can find the normal vector to P_3 using the cross product of the normal vectors to the other two planes.

$$\begin{pmatrix} 2 \\ -1 \\ 3 \end{pmatrix} \times \begin{pmatrix} 4 \\ -2 \\ 0 \end{pmatrix} = \begin{pmatrix} 6 \\ 12 \\ 0 \end{pmatrix}$$

Thus the P_3 is $\underline{6x + 12y = 12}$ (substituting R into the LHS).

ii)   Find the angle between the line RS and the plane P_3.

What is the direction of line RS? Subtracting the coordinates gives a direction vector $\begin{pmatrix} -1 \\ 3 \\ -4 \end{pmatrix}$.

Now we find the angle between this direction and the normal to P_3.

$$\begin{pmatrix} -1 \\ 3 \\ -4 \end{pmatrix} \cdot \begin{pmatrix} 6 \\ 12 \\ 0 \end{pmatrix} = -6 + 36 + 0 = 30.$$

$$30 = \sqrt{26}\sqrt{180}\cos\theta \Rightarrow \cos\theta = 0.439 \Rightarrow \theta = 64.0°$$

Thus the angle between the line and the plane is $90 - 64.0 = \underline{\mathbf{26.0°}}$

Miscellaneous Vector Questions

This page contains a variety of exam-style vector questions. To solve them you need to use a combination of the techniques listed on the preceding pages together with an intuitive feel for the 3-d situations - helped by some good, big, clear diagrams!

Find a point on the line $r = 3i + j + \lambda(2i + j + 2k)$ which is 5 units away from point A(1, 2, -1).

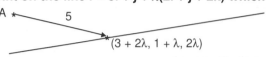

The general vector from A to the line is $\begin{pmatrix} 3+2\lambda-1 \\ 1+\lambda-2 \\ 2\lambda-(-1) \end{pmatrix} = \begin{pmatrix} 2\lambda+2 \\ \lambda-1 \\ 2\lambda+1 \end{pmatrix}$. We can find the length of this vector

using Pythagoras' Theorem, and we want it to be 5. So $(2\lambda + 2)^2 + (\lambda - 1)^2 + (2\lambda + 1)^2 = 5^2$ and this solves to give 1 or -2.111. Choosing $\lambda = 1$ for convenience, we get the point as **(5, 2, 2)**

Lines m and n have equations $\dfrac{x-1}{2} = \dfrac{y}{2}, z = 1$ and $\dfrac{x+1}{3} = \dfrac{2-y}{1} = z$

i)   **Prove the lines intersect**
ii)   **Find the Cartesian equation of the plane containing both lines.**

i)   Standard technique on page 53
ii)   Draw a diagram. How can you find the normal vector to the plane? Do you know any points on the plane?

$\underline{x - y - 4z = -3}$

This paper 2 question contains several of the techniques listed in this chapter. As before, DRAW A DIAGRAM – the points you put on do not have to bear any relation to their actual positions.

The triangle ABC has vertices at the points A(-1, 2, 3), B(-1, 3, 5) and C(0, -1, 1).
      a)   **Find the size of the angle θ between the vectors AB and AC.**
      b)   **Hence, or otherwise, find the area of triangle ABC.**
Let l_1 be the line parallel to AB which passes through D(2, -1, 0) and l_2 be the line parallel to AC which passes through E(-1, 1, 1)
      c)   i)   **Find the equations of line l_1 and l_2.**
           ii)   **Hence show that l_1 and l_2 do not intersect.**

a) <u>146.8°</u>, b) <u>2.29</u>, c) $r = \begin{pmatrix} 2 \\ -1 \\ 0 \end{pmatrix} + \lambda \begin{pmatrix} 0 \\ 1 \\ 2 \end{pmatrix}$, $r = \begin{pmatrix} -1 \\ 1 \\ 1 \end{pmatrix} + \mu \begin{pmatrix} 1 \\ -3 \\ -2 \end{pmatrix}$

STATISTICS AND PROBABILITY
Basics of Statistics

Definitions: A *population* is a set from which *statistics* are drawn. A *sample* is a subset drawn from the population. In a random sample, every member of the population is equally likely to be chosen. Sample statistics (such as the mean) can be used to estimate population statistics. *Discrete* data are restricted to certain values only (often integers) whereas *continuous* data can take any values. The *frequency* is the number of times a particular value occurs.

Presentation of Data: Numerical data is usually collected into a table and then split into *groups* or *classes*. The *boundaries* of the classes must be dealt with carefully, especially for continuous data. Consider a table of weights (see below right): into which class would a weight of 10kg be put? It would be better if the first group were labelled as $0 \leq w < 10$ and the second as $10 \leq w < 20$ and then 10 would fall into the second group. The *interval width* in this case is 10, and the *mid-interval value* of the first group is 5 and so on. Data can be appreciated more when displayed in a diagram and the *frequency histogram* is the simplest way to display grouped data. A frequency histogram (often called a *bar chart*) uses equal class intervals.

Weight (kg)
0 – 10
10 – 20

The Mean: One of the most basic statistics which can be used as a figure to represent the whole group is an average. You are required to know two different averages: the *mean* and the *median* (see page 62). To calculate the mean, add all the numbers together and divide by the number of values. So mean $= \dfrac{\sum x_i}{n}$, where the separate values are x_1, x_2, x_3 and so on. The symbol for sample mean is $\bar{x}$. Note that $n\bar{x} = \sum x_i$

If the data is in a frequency table then the total value is calculated by multiplying each value by its frequency and summing the results. (See example, right).

Pupils absent (x)	No of days (f)	fx
0	20	0
1	4	4
2	3	6
3	3	9
TOTAL	30	19

There were a total of 19 days absence over a period of 30 days. So the mean number of days absent was 19/30 = 0.63 (It is a common mistake to divide 19 by 4, the number of classes).

If the data is presented in a *grouped* frequency table, the same procedure is followed except that the mid-interval value of each group is used to represent the x value for each group. This means that the *actual* data values are unknown and in this case the mean is only an estimate.

Weight of apples (x)	No of apples (f)	Mid interval	fx
20 ≤ w < 25	12	22.5	270
25 ≤ w < 30	20	27.5	550
30 ≤ w < 35	25	32.5	812.5
35 ≤ w < 40	17	37.5	637.5
TOTAL	74		2270

Estimated mean weight of an apple is $\dfrac{2270}{4} = 30.7$

> **100 people are staying at a hotel: 68 are men and 32 women. The men have a mean height of 1.75m and the women have a mean height of 1.64m. Find the mean height of the 100 people.**
> To recalculate a mean it is always necessary to know the *total*. The total height of the men is $68 \times 1.75 = 119.0$. The total height of the women is $32 \times 1.64 = 52.48$. So the total height of *all* the people is $119 + 52.48 = 171.48$, giving a mean of $171.48/100 = \underline{\textbf{1.71m}}$

The next question asks you to tackle a topic in a way which is new. When faced with this sort of question, just carry out the mathematical techniques which are familiar and see what happens!

> **The table shows the scores of competitors in a competition.**
>
> | Score | 10 | 20 | 30 | 40 | 50 |
> |---|---|---|---|---|---|
> | Number of competitors with this score | 1 | 2 | 5 | k | 3 |
>
> **The mean score is 34. Find the value of k.**
> The total score is calculated as each score $\times$ the number of people with that score.
> $$\text{Total} = 10 + 40 + 150 + 40k + 150 = 350 + 40k.$$
> The number of competitors is $1 + 2 + 5 + k + 3 = 11 + k$
> So the mean is $\dfrac{350 + 40k}{11 + k} = 34$. To solve this equation, first cross multiply.
> $$350 + 40k = 34(11 + k)$$
> $$350 + 40k = 374 + 34k$$
> $$6k = 24 \qquad\qquad \underline{k = 4}$$

The Mode: The mode is the value that occurs the most often. In a frequency table, it is the value with the highest frequency. In a grouped frequency table, the best you can do is to say which *class* has the highest frequency – this is called the *modal class* or the *modal group*. It is perfectly possible to have more than one modal value or class.

Another measure of spread is the *range*; this is the difference between the highest and lowest values.

Standard Deviation: The mean gives an indication of the "centre" of the distribution. The next most important statistic is a measure of "spread." For example, a buyer in a crisp factory testing different packing machines would be interested to know the mean number of crisps each machine put into bags, but it is equally important to know how *consistent* the machines are. The *standard deviation* provides a measure of how much results deviate, on average, from the mean.

Although there is a formula for calculating standard deviation, you are expected to use your calculator. ▤ Make sure you understand how to enter a frequency table into your calculator and how to obtain results for the mean and standard deviation.

Try calculating the standard deviation of weight of peanuts in these 80 packets:

Weight	No of packets
$80 \le W < 85$	5
$85 \le W < 90$	10
$90 \le W < 95$	15
$95 \le W < 100$	26
$100 \le W < 105$	13
$105 \le W < 110$	7
$110 \le W < 115$	4

You should find that the mean weight is 96.8 and the standard deviation is 7.41.

As a rough indicator, the majority of results in a reasonably symmetrical distribution are within two standard deviations of the mean (ie $\mu \pm 2\sigma$).

Unbiased estimates: Generally, it is not possible to obtain statistics for a population: there may be too many, it may be too expensive or take too long to collect all the data, or members of the population may be geographically widespread. So, the population mean and SD are generally unknown, but we may want them for further calculations. The next best thing is to take a good size sample, and use the sample mean and SD as *estimates*.

- The mean of the sample is likely to be pretty close to the population mean – it is called an *unbiased estimate*.
- However, the sample size is smaller than the population and is therefore likely to have less spread; the SD is a *biased estimate* of the population SD. But we can use it to get an unbiased estimate using the formula:

$$\text{Population SD} = \sqrt{\frac{n}{n-1}} \times \text{sample SD}$$

where *n* is the sample size.

Your calculator gives both the sample SD and an estimate of population SD – which is which? Remember that populations are bigger than samples, so population SD's are bigger than sample SD's.

Variance: The variance is a useful statistic for further calculations, but does not have much significance on its own. It is the square of the standard deviation. Therefore, the formula for an unbiased estimate of population variance is:

$$\text{Population variance} = \frac{n}{n-1} \times \text{sample variance}$$

A machine makes metal bars. The lengths of 40 bars chosen at random are shown in the table below:

Length (cm)	20.0 – 20.1	20.1 – 20.2	20.2 – 20.3	20.3 – 20.4	20.4 – 20.5	20.5 – 20.6
Number of bars	2	8	12	11	6	1

Find unbiased estimates for the mean and variance of the population from which this sample was taken.

YOU SOLVE

Mean = 20.29, Variance = 0.0141

Cumulative Frequency

The median: If a set of values is listed in order, the middle value is the *median*. It is another type of average: there are as many values above the median as below it. Unlike the mean, it is unaffected by extra large or extra small values. In the following list there are 15 values so the 8th is the middle one (7 below it, 7 above it.

In general, if there are n values, the median is in the $\frac{n+1}{2}$th position.

1 1 3 5 6 6 6 **7** 7 9 10 10 12 15 18 ..... median = 7

If there is an even number of values, find the mean of the middle two to calculate the median.

24 26 27 **27 29** 30 30 33 ..... median = 28

If the data is in the form of a frequency table, then the calculation depends on whether it is discrete or continuous.

Discrete distribution

x	1	2	3	4	5	6
f	4	11	17	25	14	4

There are 75 values, so the median will be the 38th. The first 4 values are 1s, the next 11 are 2s, making 15 values so far. Another 17 are 3s making 32 values. So the 38th value must be in the next box, and thus the median is 4.

Continuous distribution

x	0 -	5 -	10 -	15 -	20 -	25 – 30
f	4	11	17	25	14	4

This time, the values are spread throughout each class, so the 38th value will be the 6th in the class $15 - 20$.

Interpolating, median $= 15 + \frac{6}{25} \times 5 = 16.2$

15   (*x values*)   20

◄─────25 items─────►

Median is 6th value of 25

Cumulative frequency tables: It is slightly easier to estimate the median from a frequency table if it is first converted into a *cumulative frequency table*. Whether the data is discrete or continuous, the method is the same. Each value of cumulative frequency measures how many x values there are in total up to that point. The two tables above convert into the following:

⊞ Beware! If you enter a grouped frequency table, you will *not* get correct values for the median and the quartiles.

x	≤ 1	≤ 2	≤ 3	≤ 4	≤ 5	≤ 6
cum. f	4	15	32	57	71	75

In this table we can see that there are 32 values up to 3, so the 38th value must be contained in the next group and is 4.

Note that in the conversion of the grouped frequency table, the "up to" points are the **top** of each group

x	<5	<10	<15	<20	<25	<30
cum. f	4	15	32	57	71	75

In the second table we have to recalculate the fact that there are 25 values in the group $15 - 20$, and then go on to the calculation shown above. The advantage here is not so great, but we can go one stage further and draw a cumulative frequency graph to help us.

The points in the table are plotted and are joined either by straight lines or a smooth curve. To find the median, a line is drawn to the right from 38 (the middle value of the distribution) and down to the x axis. The median can be seen to be about 17.

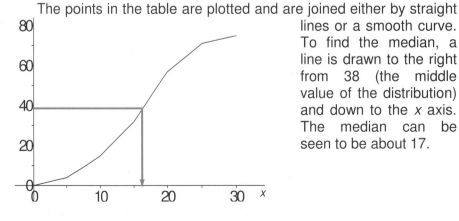

Quartiles: 50% of the population lie above the median, 50% below. We can also divide the population into *quartiles*: 25% lie below the first quartile, 50% below the second (which is also the median) 75% below the third quartile. There are 75 results in the previous table, so the first quartile will be the 19th result. Looking at the graph, this gives the first quartile as 11 and the third quartile (the 57th result) as 20. Similarly, the distribution can be divided into 100 parts knows as *percentiles*. "Your test result is in the top 5 percentiles of the population" means that at least 95% of people scored worse than you did.

Why the 19th? The median is the 38th result; the lower quartile will be the "median" of the first 37 results, ie the 19th.

Interquartile range: The standard deviation of a distribution gives us a measure of the spread of the results which is calculated using each of the values. A cruder measure of the spread is the *interquartile range* which is calculated by subtracting the lower quartile from the upper quartile. (In the question above, the IQR would be $123 - 64.5 = 58.5$). Effectively, it tells us the spread of results for the middle 50% of the population.

A survey is carried out to find the waiting times for 100 customers in a post office.

Waiting time (sec)	Number of customers		
0 – 20	5		
20 - 40	18		
40 - 60	30		
60 - 80	22		
80 - 100	9		
100 - 120	7		
120 - 140	6		
140 - 160	3		

a)   Calculate an estimate of the mean of the waiting times, by using an approximation to represent each interval. *Two extra columns have been added for you to fill in the mid-interval values and the product fx.*

b)   Construct a cumulative frequency table for these data.

c)   Use the cumulative frequency table to draw a cumulative frequency graph, using a scale of 1 cm per 20 seconds on the horizontal axis and 1 cm per 10 customers on the vertical axis.

d)   Use the cumulative frequency graph to find estimates for the median and the interquartile range.

<u>Mean = 64.4</u>, <u>Median = 50</u>, <u>IQR = 80 – 50 = 30</u>

YOU SOLVE

Box and whisker plot: A box and whisker plot is a useful device for illustrating some key statistics for a distribution. The ends of the box represent the lower and upper quartiles, and the ends of the "whiskers" the extreme values. The median is shown by a line inside the box. A scale is drawn below the box and whisker plot, and different distributions can be compared. The illustration below shows the box and whisker plots for two math exams taken by a group of students.

What do the two box plots tell you about the differences in the exam results? Try and write down three statements.

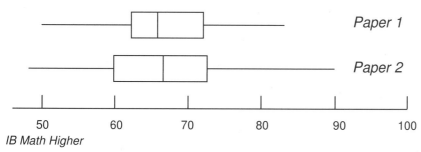

Probability Notation and Formulae

Notation: The *sample space* in a given situation is the set of all the things that can happen and is defined by the letter U. An *event* is one of the things that can happen and is given any other capital letter. A capital P stands for "probability", so we can shorten "the probability of event A" to P(A). The number of ways A can happen is denoted by $n(A)$. Probabilities are always numbers between 0 (definitely won't happen) and 1 (definitely will happen).

> In other words, to find the probability of an event, divide the number of ways it can (or did) happen by the total number of possibilities.

- $P(A) = \dfrac{n(A)}{n(U)}$

The probability that event *A* does *not* happen is denoted by *A'*. It follows that

- $P(A) + P(A') = 1$

The set notation symbols $\cap$ and $\cup$ are used for the words "and" and "or" in probability.

Combined events: The probability of event A *or* event B happening (and this includes both) is calculated using addition.

- $P(A \cup B) = P(A) + P(B)$

but this formula works **only** if A and B are *mutually exclusive* – ie they cannot both happen. If they are not mutually exclusive, use:

- $P(A \cup B) = P(A) + P(B) - P(A \cap B)$

The probability of events *A* and *B both* happening is calculated by multiplication (remember that multiplying fractions gives a *smaller* answer and it is *less* likely that both events will happen than just one).

- $P(A \cap B) = P(A) \times P(B)$

> A bag contains balls of two different colours. One is taken out, then another. The colour of the second is independent of the first if the first has been put back. If the first has been kept out, the colour of the second *depends* on the colour of the first.

but this formula works **only** if A and B are *independent* – ie one of them happening does not effect the probability of the other happening. If the events are not independent we are into the realms of *conditional probability* – ie the probability of one event happening if another has already happened. This is written as *P(A|B)*, and read as "the probability of *A* given *B*."

- $P(A|B) = \dfrac{P(A \cap B)}{P(B)}$

Note that the definition of independence is P(A) = P(A|B) = P(A|B') (in other words, the probability of *A* is the same whether or not *B* has happened). But if you are asked to test whether events are independent, just see if $P(A \cap B) = P(A) \times P(B)$.

For the events *A* and *B*, P(*A*) = 0.3, P(*B*) = 0.4.
a)   Find P(A $\cup$ B) if *A* and *B* are independent events.
b)   Find P(A' $\cap$ B') if *A* and *B* are mutually exclusive events.

In part (a) we are not told that the events are mutually exclusive, so we must use the full formula for "or". This involves $P(A \cap B)$ which we *can* calculate because we know they are independent.

So, P(A $\cap$ B) = 0.3 × 0.4 = 0.12, and P(A $\cup$ B) = P(A) + P(B) − P(A $\cap$ B) = 0.3 + 0.4 − 0.12 = **0.58**

b)   If they are mutually exclusive then P(A $\cup$ B) = 0.3 + 0.4 = 0.7 Then P(A' $\cap$ B') = 1 − 0.7 = **0.3**
Note that we cannot use independence in part (b) – this only applies to part (a)

The formulae can be quite difficult to use, so only use them if you *have* to. Many probability questions can be solved by using appropriate diagrams as shown on the next few pages.

Lists and Tables of Outcomes

Lists: A list of possible outcomes is useful if there aren't too many of them . And it is important to ensure that each outcome in the list is equally likely. For example, when three coins are thrown, the possible combinations of heads and tails are:

HHH, HHT, HTH, HTT, THH, THT, TTH, TTT

If we want to find P(exactly two heads) we can see that there are three ways of achieving this (HHT, HTH, THH) so the probability is 3/8.

Possibility Space diagram: This is a way of showing a list of outcomes on a diagram, but can only be used for two events. For example, the diagram below shows all the possible totals when two six-sided dice (red and green) are thrown:

Green						
6	7	8	9	10	11	12
5	6	7	8	9	10	11
4	5	6	7	8	9	10
3	4	5	6	7	8	9
2	3	4	5	6	7	8
1	2	3	4	5	6	7
	1	**2**	**3**	**4**	**5**	**6**

Red

Thus there are 36 possibilities. Some examples of probabilities are:

P(Total of 5) = 4/36
P(Total of 5 or 7) = 10/36
P(Total of 4 or a double) = 8/36
P(Double|total $\geq$ 9) = 2/10

> Note that there is only one way a double 2, say, can happen – a 2 on the green and a 2 on the red. But a 1 and a 3 can happen in two ways: 1 on the green and 3 on the red, or the other way around.

The conditional probability in the last example is easy to see on the diagram. We *know* that the total is $\geq$ 9, and there are 10 ways this can have happened. Of these, 2 could be a double.

Tables of outcomes: Tables of outcomes show how many ways two events can, or cannot, happen.

In a survey of 200 people, 90 of whom were female, it was found that 60 people were unemployed, including 20 males. Complete the table below. If a person is selected at random from the 200, find the probability that this person is
i)   An unemployed female.   (ii)   A male, given that the person is employed.

	Males	Females	Totals
Unemployed	20	40	60
Employed	90	50	140
Totals	110	90	200

a)   There are 40 unemployed females out of 200, so P(unemployed female) = **40/200**
b)   This is conditional probability. There are 140 employed people. Of these, 90 are males. So P(male|employed) = **90/140**

YOU SOLVE

In a survey, 100 students were asked "do you prefer to watch television or play sport?" Of the 46 boys in the survey, 33 said they preferred sport, while 29 girls made this choice. Complete the table and find the probability that:
a)   A student selected at random prefers to watch television.
b)   A student prefers to watch television, given that the student is a boy.

	Boys	Girls	Total
Television			
Sport	33	29	
Total	46		100

38/100,   13/46

Venn Diagrams

In a room there are 20 people. 11 have black hair, 6 have glasses. 2 people have both black hair and glasses. Imagine that we draw two circles on the floor labelled "black hair" and "glasses" and ask the people to stand in the appropriate circle. The circles will have to overlap to allow for the two people with both. The numbers of people in each region of the room will be:

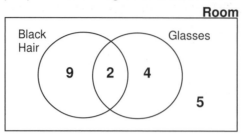

This is the same as a Venn Diagram. The "room" represents the sample space – for a particular question, there is nothing outside. Each circle represents a set, the overlap is the intersection.

A ∩ B'

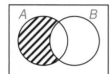

A' ∩ B'

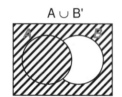

A ∪ B'

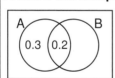

Points to note when filling in the numbers in a Venn Diagram:
- Start at the centre. If you are not told how many in the intersection, work it out like this: suppose you know there are 15 people in total in the two circles, 10 in circle A and 8 in circle B. 10 + 8 = 18, 3 more than 15 – there are 3 in the intersection.
- When we were told that there were 11 people with black hair, this *includes* those with both black hair and glasses. Same with the 6 people with glasses.
- Don't forget to fill in the outer region – although in some questions this set will be "empty."

Probabilities can now be calculated easily. When someone is selected at random, the probability they have:

Black hair and glasses = 2/20
Black hair and no glasses = 9/20
Not got glasses = 14/20
Glasses or black hair (or both) = 15/20
Glasses given black hair = 2/11
Glasses given not black hair = 4/9

A and B are independent events. P(A ∩ B) = 0.2, P(A ∩ B') = 0.3 Find P(A ∪ B).

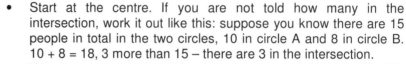

If A and B are independent, we are almost certain to be using the P(A ∩ B) = P(A) × P(B) formula at some stage. First, what can we fill into a Venn diagram? The 0.2 is in the centre, the 0.3 in the area in A but outside B. Now we can see P(A) = 0.5, so 0.2 = 0.5 × P(B) giving P(B) = 0.4. We can now complete the Venn Diagram.

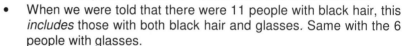

Thus, **P(A ∪ B) = 0.7**

YOU SOLVE

P(B|A) = $\frac{1}{3}$, P(B|A') = $\frac{3}{4}$, P(A) = $\frac{3}{5}$. Find P(B') and P(A|B).

Use the conditional probability formula twice to find P(B ∩ A) and P(B ∩ A'). Then draw a Venn diagram. It helps to rewrite fractions so that they have the same denominator. Or draw a tree diagram (see next page).

P(B') = 1/2, P(A|B) = 2/5

Tree Diagrams

Tree diagrams are used to work out the probabilities for a *succession* of events. To find the probability of a set of successive branches, multiply each individual probability. To find the probability of one of several branches occurring, add the probabilities of each outcome.

Note that the probabilities associated with, say, taking two balls out of a bag simultaneously are the same as if the balls were taken out consecutively.

eg: P*(rains today)* = 0.3. If it rains today, P*(rains tomorrow)* = 0.65 However, if it is dry today, P*(rains tomorrow)* = 0.2   The tree diagram which shows the full set of possible outcomes and their associated probabilities is:

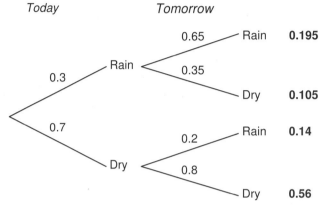

Note the following points:
- Probabilities of branches coming out of one point add to give 1 since they cover all possibilities.
- The overall probabilities also add to give 1.
- The weather tomorrow is *not* independent of the weather today, hence the different probabilities depending on today's weather.

Some example probabilities are:
- P(two rainy days) = 0.195
- P(at least one rainy day) = 0.195 + 0.105 + 0.14 = 0.44
                        = 1 − P(two dry days)
- P(exactly one rainy day) = 0.105 + 0.14 = 0.245

A bag contains 9 red balls, 10 yellow balls and 5 blue balls. Two balls are drawn at random from the bag without replacement. What is the probability that they are of different colours.

There are two events (1st ball, 2nd ball) with three outcomes each time – so you should end up with nine branches. Try to make the ends of the first set line up vertically, then the same with the ends of the second set. Remember that the probabilities for the second ball will depend on which ball was drawn out first.

Alternatively, work like this.

P(both different) = 1 − P(both same) = 1 − (P(R ∩ R) + P(Y ∩ Y) + P(B ∩ B))

185/276 = 0.670

YOU SOLVE

Discrete Probability Distributions

A probability distribution shows the probabilities for all the outcomes of a particular event. Discrete probability distributions relate to events which can only have certain outcomes – usually in the form of integers.

Note that the capital letter X is used to describe the random variable, whereas lower case x is used to represent the actual values.

Uniform distributions: If all the outcomes are equally likely, the distribution is called *uniform*. For example, here is the probability distribution for the random variable X where X represents the outcomes when throwing a die.

x	1	2	3	4	5	6
P($X = x$)	1/6	1/6	1/6	1/6	1/6	1/6

Distributions defined by a function: The following is an example of a *probability density function*:

$$P(X = x) = \begin{cases} kx, & x = 1,2,3,4,5 \\ 0 & \text{otherwise} \end{cases}$$

This means that x can only take values 1 to 5, and has probability kx for these values. The best thing to do is put all the information into a table:

x	1	2	3	4	5
P($X = x$)	k	$2k$	$3k$	$4k$	$5k$

In all probability distributions, the probabilities add to give 1, so $15k = 1$, giving $k = \frac{1}{15}$. We can fill the probabilities into the table:

x	1	2	3	4	5
P($X = x$)	$\frac{1}{15}$	$\frac{2}{15}$	$\frac{3}{15}$	$\frac{4}{15}$	$\frac{5}{15}$

Expected values of distribution parameters: We can now calculate what we expect to happen when the trials take place. The more trials that are carried out, the closer the observed statistics will get to the expected ones.

- *Expected mean (expectation)* $= \sum xp$. Simply multiply each pair of values along the table. In the example, this gives $\frac{55}{15} = 3.67$

- *Expected variance* $= \sum x^2 p - \bar{x}^2$. Remember this as the "expectation of the squares – the square of the expectation." Work through the example; you should get 15.

- *Expected standard deviation* is the square root of the expected variance; in this case, $\sqrt{15} = 3.87$.

- *Expected mode* is the value with the highest probability: 5.

- *Expected median* is the value which you have an equal probability of getting above or below. We can see from the table that the 50:50 split comes when $x = 4$. ($\frac{7\frac{1}{2}}{15}$ both sides!)

YOU SOLVE

The probability distribution for a random variable x is given by:

P($X = x$) = $kx(x – 1)$, for x = 2, 3, 4, 5, 6

i) Find the value of k.

ii) Find the expected mean and variance of the distribution.

Begin by drawing up a probability table.

$k = 1/70$, $E(X) = 5$, $var(X) = 1.2$

Binomial Distribution

The Binomial probably distribution is a special case of a discrete distribution. You can use it when:

- There are a fixed number of "trials"
- Each trial has only two possible outcomes, "success" and "failure."
- The results of each trial are independent of each other.
- The probability of success remains the same.

For example, my young child wakes me up 1 night in 4. I want to find the probability that I will be woken up 3 nights out of 10.

- The number of trials, n, is 10.
- The probability of "success" (ie being woken up!) is 0.25
- We therefore say that the distribution is $X \sim B(10, 0.25)$

The calculation has three parts to it:

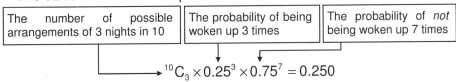

The number of possible arrangements of 3 nights in 10	The probability of being woken up 3 times	The probability of *not* being woken up 7 times

$$^{10}C_3 \times 0.25^3 \times 0.75^7 = 0.250$$

Thus there are always three parts to a binomial probability calculation *except* when you are at either end of the distribution. In which case: P(woken up all 10 nights) = 0.25^{10}; and the probability of not being woken up at all in ten nights is 0.75^{10}.

Actually, $^{10}C_{10} \times .25^{10} \times .75^0$

Getting the probability: You may simply be given the probability of success, or:

- You calculate the probability from previous experience (as in the example above)
- You calculate it from your knowledge of the situation (eg: success is getting a 2 on the spinner: p = 1/3.
- The probability is the result of a calculation from a previous part of the question.

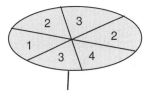

---

350 of the 500 pupils in a school have the letter "s" in their name. If 6 pupils are chosen at random, what is the probability that 4 of them have an "s" in their name.

P("s") = 350/500 = 0.7. Therefore, $X \sim B(6, 0.7)$. P(4 successes) = $^6C_4 \times 0.7^4 \times 0.3^2 = $ **0.324**

More than one outcome: Since binomial probabilities are all mutually exclusive (I cannot be woken up both 3 nights *and* 4 nights in 10), the probability of one of several outcomes occurring can be found by addition. Thus, P(I am woken up 3 or 4 nights out of 10) = $^{10}C_3 \times 0.25^3 \times 0.75^7 + {}^{10}C_4 \times 0.25^4 \times 0.75^6 = 0.396$.

Many calculators will be able to calculate binomial probabilities for you. But you must enter the data in the correct order.

Check the wording of questions carefully. It might say: "Find the probability that I have at least eight nights when I am *not* woken up." Check this also gives 0.526.

Cumulative probabilities: What is the probability of being woken up on fewer than 3 nights out of 10: that is, P(0, 1, or 2). You can add these three probabilities together or use the cumulative probability function on your calculator which gives 0.526. This enables us to answer questions such as: "Find the probability that I am awoken on at least 3 nights out of 10."

Nights awoken	0	1	2	3	4	5	6	7	8	9	10

want this →

← Total probability = 1 →

The diagram shows that the easiest way to calculate this is to find the cumulative probability up to 2, and subtract the answer from 1. This gives $1 - 0.526 = 0.474$.

Mean and standard deviation: Fortunately, we do not have to go through the normal process for discrete distributions – there are two simple formulae for binomial distributions. If n is the number of trials, p the probability of success and q the probability of failure, then:

- Mean = np
- Standard deviation = $\sqrt{npq}$

It is thought that 60% of the people in a town have been vaccinated against smallpox. Tests on a random sample of 200 show that only one half have been vaccinated. Does this throw doubt on the original belief?

Each person either has or has not been vaccinated, and we assume that people are vaccinated independently (this is arguable). Thus we have a binomial distribution. If X is the number of people vaccinated, $X \sim B(200, 0.6)$

The mean is 120 (the number of people we would *expect* to have been vaccinated). The standard deviation is 6.93. Generally, we expect a result in the range $\mu \pm 2\sigma$, that is from 106 to 133. 100 is outside this range, and therefore we can conclude that probably fewer than 60% have been vaccinated.

YOU SOLVE

A machine contains a critical component. This component is replicated 10 times within the machine, and the machine works as long as at least one of the ten components is working. Each has an independent probability of failing within one year of 0.7, and all the components are replaced at the end of a year.
a)   Find the probability that all 10 fail within the year.
Be careful with the words success and failure – in this case, a failing component is a probability success!

b)   Find the probability that the machine is in operation at the end of the year.

c)   Suppose we put in n components. What is the probability that the machine is operating at the end of the year? Hence find the smallest number of components to install which will ensure a probability of at least 0.99 that the machine is working at the end of the year. *For the first part, look at how you got the answers to parts (a) and (b).*

a) <u>0.0282</u>   b) <u>0.9718</u>   c) <u>$1 - 0.7^n$</u>   <u>$n \geq 12$</u>

Poisson Distribution

Conditions for a Poisson distribution: A random variable has a Poisson distribution if the following conditions are fulfilled:

- The variable is discrete
- The occurrences are random
- The occurrences are independent
- There is a known mean rate for the occurrences

Examples of events which might be modelled by a Poisson distribution are: the number of telephone calls a switchboard receives in a 5 minute period; the number of deaths per year from lightning strikes.

Calculating Poisson probabilities: One of the main features of the Poisson distribution is that the mean is equal to the variance. The symbol used for both is μ, so

$$E(X) = Var(X) = \mu$$

To calculate the probability that $X = r$:

$$P(X = r) = \frac{\mu^r e^{-\mu}}{r!}, \text{ for } \mu > 0 \text{ and } r = 0, 1, \ldots$$

In practice you may find it easier to use your calculator to find Poisson probabilities.

It is unlikely that μ will be greater than 20 in a Poisson distribution question – there are easier ways to deal with these larger parameters.

Cumulative probabilities: The telephone switchboard above has a mean of 4.4 calls in a 5 minute period. If we want to find the probability of 2 or fewer calls in 5 minutes, the calculation will be:

$$\frac{4.4^0 e^{-4.4}}{0!} + \frac{4.4^1 e^{-4.4}}{1!} + \frac{4.4^2 e^{-4.4}}{2!} = 0.185$$

If we have been asked to find the probability of *more* than 2 calls in a 5 minute period, this can be calculated as $1 - 0.185 = 0.815$.

Weak spots occur at random in the manufacture of a certain type of rope at an average rate of 2 per 100 metres. If X represents the number of weak spots in 100 metres of cable, write down the distribution of X.

The weak spots occur at random and, presumably, independently of each other. Thus we can say that the distribution is Poisson. **$X \sim P(2)$**

Lengths of rope are wound onto drums. Each drum carries 60m of rope. Find the probability that the drum will have 4 or more weak spots.

For 60m, $\mu = 0.6 \times 2 = 1.2$. We need to calculate $1 - P(X < 4)$

$$P(X < 4) = \frac{1.2^0 e^{-1.2}}{0!} + \frac{1.2^1 e^{-1.2}}{1!} + \frac{1.2^2 e^{-1.2}}{2!} + \frac{1.2^3 e^{-1.2}}{3!} = 0.966$$

Thus, $P(X \geq 4) = 1 - 0.966 = \underline{\textbf{0.034}}$ *(Or use cumulative tables or your GDC).*

A contractor buys 5 such drums. Find the probability that just two have one weak spot each.

P(one weak spot in a drum) $= 1.2e^{-1.2} = 0.3614$. Each drum either has a weak spot or it doesn't – so we now have a Binomial distribution. $W \sim B(5, 0.3614)$ (where W is the number of drums with a weak spot).

$$P(W = 2) = {}^5C_2 (0.3614)^2 (0.6386)^3 = \underline{\textbf{0.340}}$$

Continuous Distributions

Continuous random variables: Phone calls from an office last between 0 and 5 minutes. The time forms a *continuous random variable*: continuous because any value in the range can occur; random because there is no predictable pattern. The probability might be modelled by a function:

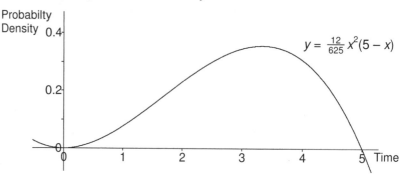

The values on the y axis are not probability, but *probability density*. On its own, fairly meaningless, but you've got to call the axis something!

The important thing is that AREA = PROBABILITY. That accounts for the $\frac{12}{625}$ - it ensures that the total area under the graph is 1. In some questions this constant is written as k and you are asked to work it out. Just integrate the function over the appropriate range and put the result equal to 1.

Find the probability that a call lasts between 2 and 3 minutes.

The probability is $\int_2^3 \frac{12}{625} x^2(5-x)dx = \mathbf{0.296}$

Mode: The mode, the most likely expected value, is the maximum point on the graph. From the calculator, this occurs when $x = 3.33$, ie 3.33 minutes is the most likely time for a call.

Median: The expected median will occur at the point which exactly divides the area under the graph into two equal parts. We therefore need to solve the equation $\int_0^m \frac{12}{625} x^2(5-x)dx = 0.5$ for m.

You cannot use your calculator for this, so try integrating "by hand." You should arrive at the equation $40m^3 - 6m^4 - 625 = 0$, which has a solution $m = 3.07$ minutes. This is the median value: you are likely to have as many phone calls below this time as above it.

The limits are always replaced by the appropriate range in any question; in this case, 0 to 5.

Mean: In general, the expected mean of a continuous distribution is found using the formula $\mu = \int_{-\infty}^{\infty} xf(x)dx$. So, just multiply the probability density function by x and integrate. In our example, this gives the mean as 3 minutes.

Compare these formulae with those for discrete distributions on page 66.

Variance: The formula for the expected variance is $\int_{-\infty}^{\infty} x^2 f(x)dx - \mu^2$. This gives exactly 1, and hence the standard deviation is also 1.

Function definition: The probability density function will be defined in a specific format. The above example would be written as:

$$f(x) = \begin{cases} \frac{12}{625} x^2(5-x), & 0 \leq x \leq 5 \\ 0, & \text{elsewhere} \end{cases}$$

A probability density function for the life *t* hours of an Osmarc light bulb is given as:

$$f(x) = \begin{cases} ke^{\frac{-t}{1200}}, & t > 0 \\ 0 & \text{elsewhere} \end{cases}.$$

a) Find the value of the constant *k*.
b) Find the probability that a bulb will last more than 2000 hours.
c) Find the age beyond which only 10% of Osmarc bulbs survive.

Being an exponential graph, the *x* axis will be an asymptote, so there is no upper limit. Remember this is only a *model* for the real-life situation.

a) $\int_0^\infty ke^{\frac{-t}{1200}} dt = 1 \Rightarrow k\left[-1200 e^{\frac{-t}{1200}} \right]_0^\infty = 1$

$k(0 - (-1200)) = 1$

So **k = 1/1200**   *(Better to keep the fraction than use recurring decimals)*

b)   We can now substitute the value of *k* into the function:

$$P(t > 1200) = \frac{1}{1200}\left[-1200 e^{\frac{-t}{1200}} \right]_{2000}^\infty = \underline{\textbf{0.189}}$$

Note that we have not had to do the integral again.

c)   We now need to find the value of *t* above which there is an area of 0.1.

$$\frac{1}{1200}\left[-1200 e^{\frac{-t}{1200}} \right]_T^\infty = 0.1 \Rightarrow e^{\frac{-T}{1200}} = 0.1$$

This leads to the equation *T* = -1200ln0.1 = 2763, so **10% of bulbs last more than 2763 hours**

Quite often, particularly in longer questions, you are asked to use a probability found from a continuous distribution as the probability of "success" in a binomial distribution – ie a completely new question.

The time, in hours, that William is likely to spend on his maths assignment (on a sunny Sunday) is represented by the continuous random variable X which has probability density function: $f(x) = \begin{cases} e - ke^{kx}, & 0 \le x \le 1 \\ 0 & \text{otherwise} \end{cases}$.

a) Show that *k* = 1.
Two points here. Note the word "show". You don't have to find k; just substitute k = 1 into the integral and show the total area is 1 as a result. And be careful integrating e; remember that it is a constant, like 2.

b) Find in terms of *e* the mean of the distribution. *You will need integration by parts.*

e/2 - 1

c) Find the probability that Bill spends more than 30 minutes on his assignment.

0.2896

d) What is the probability that Bill spends less than 30 minutes on his assignment on exactly 2 out of 3 sunny Sundays? What assumption must you make?

0.438,   Assume the amount of time spent is independent each time

YOU SOLVE

The Normal Distribution

The Normal Distribution is a continuous distribution which is used to model many commonly occurring frequency distributions, eg: the heights of trees, weights of people. The curve has the following properties:

- It is symmetrical about the mean value, μ.
- The median is the same as the mean.
- The curve approaches the x-axis asymptotically (although this is not true for the majority of distributions the curve is modelling).

The curve (shown on the left) is called the *standard* normal distribution: its mean is 0, its standard deviation is 1 and the area under the curve is 1. We can use either tables or calculator to find an area under the curve between two x values – and this represents the probability that a value lies in that range. If we use the tables we must *standardise* the real-life statistics. If $X \sim N(\mu, \sigma^2)$ - ie X forms a Normal Distribution with mean μ and standard deviation σ - then the standardised value of X is calculated as $Z = \dfrac{X - \mu}{\sigma}$. So, the procedure for calculating normal probabilities is to first standardise the value of X, draw a diagram to see which area we are interested in, then use tables to find the probability. Several examples are set out below to show various cases, and how to lay out the working. The symbol Φ is used when looking up the area.

For example, a group of people have heights which are normally distributed with μ = 160cm, σ = 10cm. We are interested in those with a height over 165cm – this becomes a *standardised* value of 0.5 since 165 is 0.5 standard deviations above the mean.

The divisions on the x axis are each 0.5 of a standard deviation.

🖩 You should be able to solve Normal probability problems using calculator functions, and using the Normal probability tables

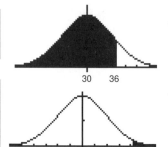

$X \sim N(30, 5^2)$. Find P($X \le 36$).
- $Z = (36 - 30)/5 = 1.2$
- $P(X \le 36) = \Phi(1.2) = \underline{0.8849}$

$X \sim N(120, 100)$. Find $P(X \ge 141)$.
- $Z = (141 - 120)/10 = 2.1$
- $P(X \ge 141) = 1 - \Phi(2.1) = \underline{0.0179}$

If the value of X is to the *left* of the mean, we use the symmetry of the curve to calculate the area.

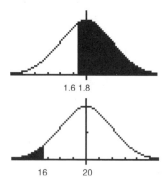

$X \sim N(1.8, 0.6^2)$. Find P($X \ge 1.6$)
- This is the same as P(≤ 2.0)
- $Z = (2.0 - 1.8)/0.6 = 0.333$
- $P(X \ge 1.6) = \Phi(0.333) = \underline{0.6306}$

$X \sim N(20, 12)$. Find P($X \le 16$)
- This is the same as P($X \ge 24$)
- $Z = (24 - 20)/\sqrt{12} = 1.16$
- $P(X \le 16) = 1 - \Phi(1.16) = \underline{0.124}$

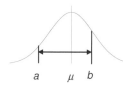

If you need to find the area *between* two values, treat the problem as two separate questions, perhaps drawing separate diagrams. Find the area up to a, then the area up to b, then subtract.

We have used $Z = \dfrac{X - \mu}{\sigma}$ to standardise values of X. However, as with any formula, you may already have Z and are required to calculate, say, μ. It is likely that you will not be given Z directly: you may have to use the tables "backwards" (or the equivalent operation on the calculator) to find Z. For example, you may be told that 30% of a certain group of people have a weight over 80kg. Using the tables backwards, we find what value of Z gives an area of 0.7 – this is 0.525.

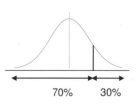

70%　30%

Suppose we are now told that the value of σ is 15 and require the value of μ.

$$0.525 = \frac{80 - \mu}{15}$$
$$\mu = 80 - 15 \times 0.525$$
$$= 72.1$$

This idea can translate into questions such as this:

In a certain exam, 12% of candidates were ungraded. If the mean mark was 52% and the standard deviation was 13, what is the highest mark which a candidate could obtain and not gain a grade, assuming marks are integers?

12%　88%

The diagram shows that the bottom 12% must be to the left of the mean. Using the symmetry of the graph, the area below the line would become the area *above* the line when reflected. So, to find the standardised value, we use the tables backwards for 88%. This gives $Z = 1.175$.

So, $-1.175 = \dfrac{X - 52}{13} \Rightarrow x = 36.7$

The highest possible ungraded mark is therefore **36%**.

Note the use of the minus sign: on a standardised normal distribution the mean is 0, so all standardised values to the left are negative. In other words, our mark is 1.175 standard deviations *below* the mean.

General points when solving Normal Distribution questions.
- Sort out first exactly what the question is asking. Have you been given the percentage or proportion of the population involved: if so, you are going to have to work backwards.
- Always draw a rough sketch. It may help to put separate rows underneath for X and Z values, and double headed arrows or shading for area. A sketch will also be your "working" when you use the GDC to calculate probabilities.
- Use the formula and fill in what you know.
- Check you have answered exactly what the question asked.
- Make sure your answer is sensible. For example, if you have been asked to calculate a mean, does your answer fall nicely in the middle of your diagram?

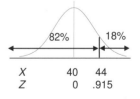

82%　18%

| X | 40 | 44 |
| Z | 0 | .915 |

Here is the solution for a complete section B question:

Note that you will <u>always</u> be told if a distribution is Normal.

A machine is set to produce bags of salt, whose weights are distributed normally, with a mean of 110g and standard deviation of 1.142g. If the weight of a bag of salt is less than 108g, the bag is rejected. With these settings, 4% of the bags are rejected.

The settings of the machine are altered and it is found that 7% of the bags are rejected.

a) (i) If the mean has not changed, find the new SD, correct to 3 decimal places.

What has happened is that the alteration to the machine has made it less accurate; the weights are more spread out, so more fall below 108g.

The calculator tells us that an area of 0.07 is equivalent to a standardised value of −1.4758 (use 4DP to get an accurate answer to 3DP) This can now be put into the standardising formula – a pivotal hinge between the calculations and the graph.

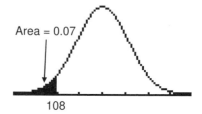

Area = 0.07

108

$-1.4758 = \dfrac{108-110}{\sigma} \Rightarrow \sigma = 1.355$, slightly more than before, as we suspected. So, **<u>new standard deviation = 1.355g</u>**

(ii) Find the value, correct to 2 decimal places, at which the mean should be set so that only 4% of the bags are rejected.

So now, accepting that we cannot improve the spread of results, we are going to increase the mean slightly (by putting more salt in each bag) and thus reduce the rejection rate. We still reject bags below 108g.

An area of 0.04 is equivalent to $z = -1.751$.

$-1.751 = \dfrac{108-\mu}{1.355} \Rightarrow \mu = 110.37$, a very slight increase. Now you can see why we are working to such accuracy. Thus, **<u>new mean = 110.37g</u>**

b) With the new settings from part (a), it is found that 80% of the bags of salt have a weight which lies between Ag and Bg, where A and B are symmetric about the mean. Find the values of A and B, giving your answers correct to two decimal places.

Look at the diagram. If the shaded area is 80%, then 40% is above the mean. So the *total* area up to B must be 90% (50 + 40).

Area = 0.8

An area of 0.9 is equivalent to $Z = 1.2816$.

A B

$1.2816 = \dfrac{B-110.37}{1.355} \Rightarrow B = 112.11$.

We can then use symmetry to find A (because it is the same distance the other side of the mean).

Thus, **<u>$A = 108.63$, $B = 112.11$</u>**

CALCULUS
Differentiation – The Basics

Suppose we know that the rate of inflation is 3%. This fact is useful, but would be more useful if we knew how it was changing. If its rate of change is down 0.1%/month, we can make a guess at the rate of inflation in 6 months' time. Similarly, it is useful to know we are 100km from our destination, even more useful if we know our rate of change of distance (ie speed) is 60kmh^{-1}. The process of finding a "rate of change function" for a given function is called differentiation. You need to know the rules for differentiating different types of function, and for differentiating composite functions.

> The *gradient* of a graph at a point represents the rate of change of the function – so differentiation gives us the gradient of a graph at any point.

Notation: When you differentiate a function, the new function (the gradient function) is called the *derived* function (or *derivative*). If the original function is f(x), the derived function is written as f'(x). Alternatively, if the function is written in the form $y = f(x)$, the derived function is denoted by $\frac{dy}{dx}$.

> Don't confuse:
> f'(x) Derived function
> f^{-1}(x) Inverse function

Differentiating different types of function: You need to be able to differentiate various types of function (see table on right). If any functions are added or subtracted they can be differentiated independently. That is, f(x) ± g(x) differentiated is f'(x) ± g'(x). This will not work for multiplication or division (eg to differentiate $(x + 1)(x - 2)$ you must first multiply out the brackets).

If a function is multiplied or divided by a *constant*, however, the constant just sits there: eg $2x^3$ differentiated is $2 \times 3x^2 = 6x^2$.

Also remember that functions of the form kx differentiate to give k, and that constants (which have a zero rate of change) differentiate to give 0.

f(x)	f'(x)
x^n	nx^{n-1}
$\sin x$	$\cos x$
$\cos x$	$-\sin x$
$\tan x$	$\sec^2 x$
e^x	e^x
$\ln(x)$	$1/x$
$\sin^{-1} x$	$\dfrac{1}{\sqrt{1-x^2}}$
$\cos^{-1} x$	$-\dfrac{1}{\sqrt{1-x^2}}$
$\tan^{-1} x$	$\dfrac{1}{1+x^2}$

Differentiating x^n: x^n differentiates to give nx^{n-1} for all $n \in \mathbb{Q}$.

This allows us to differentiate reciprocal and root functions. First, remember to write these functions as powers and with x in the numerator. Examples are:

$x^2 - 3x$	$2x - 3$
$x^3 - 4$	$3x^2$
$2x(x - 1)$	$4x - 2$

f(x)	f(x) rewritten	f'(x)	f'(x) simplified
$\sqrt{x}$	$x^{\frac{1}{2}}$	$\dfrac{1}{2}x^{-\frac{1}{2}}$	$\dfrac{1}{2\sqrt{x}}$
$\dfrac{4}{x^2}$	$4x^{-2}$	$-8x^{-3}$	$\dfrac{-8}{x^3}$
$x\sqrt{x}$	$x^{\frac{3}{2}}$	$\dfrac{3}{2}x^{\frac{1}{2}}$	$\dfrac{3\sqrt{x}}{2}$
$\dfrac{2}{\sqrt{x}}$	$2x^{-\frac{1}{2}}$	$-\dfrac{1}{2} \times 2x^{-\frac{3}{2}}$	$\dfrac{-1}{x^{\frac{3}{2}}}$

Differentiating sin$x$, cos$x$ and tan$x$: x must be in radians for these differentiations to give correct results. eg: What is the gradient of the graph of $y = x + \sin x$ when $x = 1$? $\frac{dy}{dx} = 1 + \cos x$ so when $x = 1$, the gradient is $1 + \cos 1 = 1.54$. With the calculator set in degrees, you would get 1.9998.

Differentiation from First Principles

What is it? It is fortunate that there are fairly simples rules and patterns for remembering how to differentiate most functions. Differentiating from first principles is a method, based on consideration of tangents, which enables us to find the differential of any function without using any rules or patterns. It requires an understanding of the idea of a *limit*.

x	$f(x)$
10	1.5454...
100	1.9505...
1000	1.9950...
10000	1.9995...

Limits: What value does the function $f(x) = \dfrac{2x-3}{x+1}$ tend to as x gets very large? The table on the left suggests that f(x) tends towards 2; by considering the function, we can see that as x gets very large, the 3 and the 1 become insignificant, and we are indeed left with f(x) = 2. This can be written as $\lim_{x\to\infty} f(x) = 2$, read as: "The limit of f(x) as x tends to infinity is 2." (We also meet the idea of a limit when we consider the sum of a GP). x will never *reach* infinity, but if we think of infinity as a real place – off the map, perhaps – then the function would get to 2.

A good analogy is speed. The average speed of a car which takes 2 hours to travel 140km is 70kmh^{-1}. But at a given instant, its speed might be 85 kmh^{-1}: this only means that if the car were to continue at that speed, it would travel 85km in the next hour.

Average gradient v. instantaneous gradient: The average gradient between two points is the change in y divided by the change in x. The instantaneous gradient is the gradient of the tangent at a single point.

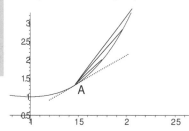

How can we calculate the gradient at a point? On the left is part of the graph of $f(x) = x^3 - 2x^2 + x +1$. We can find the gradient of the tangent at A (dotted line) by drawing a succession of lines to points above A, but getting closer to A, calculate the average gradients and see what they tend to. The process can be formalised into a general formula (note that h indicates a small distance in the x direction):

The gradient of the line from A to B is $\dfrac{f(x+h)-f(x)}{h}$. As B slides down the curve towards A, this gradient gets closer to the gradient of the tangent at A and this, of course, is the *derivative* at A. Thus we can write:

$$f'(x) = \lim_{h\to 0} \frac{f(x+h)-f(x)}{h}.$$

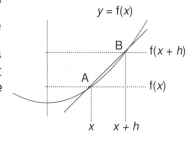

Doing the calculation: To differentiate from first principles for a specific function, all you need to do is substitute into the above formula. The key part of the working, however, is to <u>simplify the top line</u>, otherwise you end up with 0/0.

You will also need to be able to differentiate sin*x* and cos*x* from first principles.

Differentiate $f(x) = x^2 - 2x$ from first principles.

$f(x+h) - f(x) = ((x+h)^2 - 2(x+h)) - (x^2 - 2x)$

Multiplying out and simplifying: $x^2 + 2xh + h^2 - 2x - 2h - x^2 + 2x = 2xh - 2h + h^2$

Factorising, we get: $h(2x - 2 + h)$

Now we substitute into the formula: $f'(x) = \lim_{x\to 0} \dfrac{h(2x-2+h)}{h} = \lim_{x\to 0}(2x - 2 + h)$

All we now have to do is put $h = 0$ to get $\underline{f'(x) = 2x - 2}$

The Chain Rule

The Chain Rule is used to differentiate composite functions. Consider the function $y = (4x + 3)^2$ If we write the "inner function" (ie $4x + 3$) as a single letter u, then the function becomes $y = u^2$. The chain rule shows us how the rates of change of *three* variables (as opposed to two) are connected:

$$\frac{dy}{dx} = \frac{dy}{du} \times \frac{du}{dx}$$

We can then use the chain rule like this:

$$u = 4x + 3 \qquad \frac{du}{dx} = 4$$

$$y = u^2 \qquad \frac{dy}{du} = 2u$$

$$\frac{dy}{dx} = \frac{dy}{du} \times \frac{du}{dx} = 2u \times 4 = 8u = 8(4x + 3)$$

An alternative, informal, method is to proceed as follows:
- Take the "inner function" (in brackets) and differentiate it: 4
- Work out the "outer function" differentiated: $(...)^2 \to 2(...)$
- Multiply the two together: $8(...)$
- Fill in the brackets: $8(4x + 3)$

More examples using the informal method are shown on the right.

A "3 link chain" is best done using the formal method. eg: To differentiate $\cos^3 4x$, let $v = 4x$, let $u = \cos v$ and then $y = u^3$. Then

$$\frac{dy}{dx} = \frac{dy}{du} \times \frac{du}{dv} \times \frac{dv}{dx} = 3u^2 \times (-\sin v) \times 4 = -12 \sin 4x \cos^2 4x$$

Differentiating reciprocal functions: The chain rule can be used to find the derivatives of functions of the form $\frac{1}{f(x)}$ since these can be written as $[f(x)]^{-1}$. In particular, this enables us to differentiate $\sec x$, $\csc x$ and $\cot x$. For example:

If $f(x) = \csc x$ then $f(x) = (\sin x)^{-1}$. $f'(x) = \cos x \times -(\sin x)^{-2} = -\dfrac{\cos x}{\sin^2 x}$

(Show that this is the same as $-\csc x \cot x$)

$f(x) = \cos(2x - 4)$
Inner function is $2x - 4$
Differentiate inner $\to 2$
Differentiate $\cos(...) \to -\sin(...)$
Multiply $-2\sin(...)$
Result: $f'(x) = -2\sin(2x - 4)$

$f(x) = \ln(1 + x^2)$
Inner function is $1 + x^2$
Differentiate inner $\to 2x$
Differentiate $\ln(...) = 1/(...)$
Multiply $2x \times 1/(...)$
Result: $f'(x) = 2x/(1 + x^2)$

$f(x) = \sqrt{1 - 5x} = (1 - 5x)^{\frac{1}{2}}$
Inner function is $1 - 5x$
Differentiate inner $\to -5$
Differentiate $(...)^{1/2} \to \frac{1}{2}(...)^{-\frac{1}{2}}$
Multiply $-\frac{5}{2}(...)^{-\frac{1}{2}}$
Result: $f'(x) = -\frac{5}{2}(1 - 5x)^{-\frac{1}{2}}$

$f(x) = e^{x^3} = e^{(x^3)}$
Inner function is x^3
Differentiate inner $\to 3x^2$
Differentiate $e^{(...)} \to e^{(...)}$
Multiply $3x^2 \times e^{(...)}$
Result: $f'(x) = 3x^2(e^{x^2})$

> **Let $f(x) = \cos x$ and $g(x) = 2x^2$. Find expressions for $(g \circ f)(x)$ and $(f \circ g)'(x)$.**
>
> $(g \circ f)(x) = g(f(x)) = g(\cos x) = \underline{\mathbf{2(\cos x)^2}}$
>
> $(f \circ g)(x) = f(g(x)) = f(2x^2) = \cos(2x^2)$ We now need to differentiate this to get $(f \circ g)'(x)$. Because it is a composite function, we use the chain rule.
>   Inner function $= 2x^2$ which differentiates to $4x$.
>   Outer function is $\cos(...)$ which differentiates to $-\sin(...)$ So, $(f \circ g)'(x) = \underline{\mathbf{-4x\sin(2x^2)}}$

> **If $f(x) = e^{(1 + \sin \pi x)}$, find $f'(x)$.**
>
>
> $\pi \cos \pi x\, e^{(1 + \sin \pi x)}$

Differentiating a^x: $a^x = e^{x \ln a}$ (since $e^{x \ln a} = e^{\ln a^x} = a^x$) This can be differentiated using the chain rule:

$$\frac{d}{dx}(a^x) = \ln a \times e^{x \ln a} = a^x \ln a$$

Remember that $\ln a$ is a constant.

Product and Quotient Rules

When you have to differentiate two functions multiplied together you must use the *product rule*; and when two functions are divided, you must use the *quotient rule*. If the two functions are $u(x)$ and $v(x)$ – normally shortened to u and v – then the rules are:

How can you tell the difference between a composite function and a product of functions? In a composite function x only appears once; in a product x appears twice.

- PRODUCT RULE: $\quad \dfrac{d}{dx}(uv) = u\dfrac{dv}{dx} + v\dfrac{du}{dx}$

- QUOTIENT RULE: $\quad \dfrac{d}{dx}\left(\dfrac{u}{v}\right) = \dfrac{v\dfrac{du}{dx} - u\dfrac{dv}{dx}}{v^2}$

It may be helpful to think of the rules more informally as:

Product Rule:
(1st fn × 2nd fn differentiated) + (2nd fn × 1st fn differentiated)

Quotient Rule:
$\dfrac{\text{(bottom × top differentiated) - (top × bottom differentiated)}}{\text{bottom line squared}}$

Another quick way to remember them:

Product Rule is $uv' + vu'$
Quotient Rule is $\dfrac{vu' - uv'}{v^2}$

(the ' means "differentiate")

Note the + in the product rule and the − in the quotient rule. Also remember that, because of the minus sign, the order is important in the quotient rule.

When you are asked to do these more complicated differentiations, you can either write down every step in the formulae (safe but time-consuming) or you can do some of it in your head (faster, but you can go wrong). Here is an example of full working:

Differentiate $y = x^2 \sin x$

$$u = x^2 \qquad \frac{du}{dx} = 2x$$

$$v = \sin x \qquad \frac{dv}{dx} = \cos x$$

$$\frac{dy}{dx} = u\frac{dv}{dx} + v\frac{du}{dx} = x^2 \cos x + 2x \sin x$$

It is possible that either (or both, if you are unlucky) of u and v are composite functions, in which case you will have to use the chain rule as well.

Differentiate $y = \sin(2x + 3)/x^2$

$$u = \sin(2x + 3) \qquad \frac{du}{dx} = 2\cos(2x + 3)$$

$$v = x^2 \qquad \frac{dv}{dx} = 2x$$

$$\frac{dy}{dx} = \frac{v\dfrac{du}{dx} - u\dfrac{dv}{dx}}{v^2} = \frac{2x^2 \cos(2x+3) - 2x\sin(2x+3)}{x^4}$$

Like many quotient rule differentiations, this can be simplified by factorising the top line, then dividing through by x. Try it.

Once you have differentiated, don't forget that the end result is – as before – the rate of change of the original function, the gradient of the graph at any point.

Differentiating $\log_a x$: Using the rule for changing the base of a logarithm, we can rewrite $\log_a x$ as $\dfrac{\ln x}{\ln a}$. This looks like a quotient rule, but since $\ln a$ is a constant, it differentiates simply to give $\dfrac{1}{x \ln a}$

Second Derivative

Notation: When a function is differentiated a second time, use the notation $\dfrac{d^2y}{dx^2}$ or $f''(x)$.

Interpretation: The first derivative gives us the gradient function, so the second derivative gives us the "rate of change of gradient" function. If, for example, $f''(3) = 2$ this means that when $x = 3$, the gradient of the graph is increasing at a rate of 2 (for every increase in x of 1). It does not necessarily mean that the gradient itself is positive – only that it is increasing. This tells us about the shape of the curve. The diagram below shows what happens for various values of the first and second derivatives and covers every possible point on any curve.

	$\dfrac{dy}{dx} < 0$	$\dfrac{dy}{dx} = 0$	$\dfrac{dy}{dx} > 0$
$\dfrac{d^2y}{dx^2} < 0$		MAXIMUM	
$\dfrac{d^2y}{dx^2} = 0$	POINTS OF INFLEXION		
$\dfrac{d^2y}{dx^2} > 0$		MINIMUM	

Note the following:
- For a point of inflexion to occur $f''(x) = 0$, but the gradient at a point of inflexion is not necessarily 0.
- A point where $f''(x) = 0$ is not necessarily a point of inflexion. For example, $y = x^4$ has a *minimum* when $f''(x) = 0$.
- The sign of the second derivative at a turning point identifies the nature of the point: a maximum if $f''(x) < 0$, a minimum if $f''(x) > 0$.

Use the product rule to find and identify the stationary point on the graph of $f(x) = xe^{-x}$

(Note that we must use the product rule, so we can only use a calculator as a check)

$$f'(x) = x(-e^{-x}) + 1 \times (e^{-x}) = -xe^{-x} + e^{-x}$$

For stationary points, $f'(x) = 0$, so $-xe^{-x} + e^{-x} = 0 \Rightarrow e^{-x}(-x + 1) = 0 \Rightarrow \mathbf{x = 1}$

We also need the y-coordinate. When $x = 1$, $f(1) = e^{-1}$, so SP is at $\mathbf{(1, e^{-1})}$

To identify the nature of the stationary point we differentiate again. We note that the first part of the function $f'(x)$ is the same as $f(x)$, but with a minus sign. So it will give the same derivative, with a minus sign. $f''(x) = -(-xe^{-x} + e^{-x}) - e^{-x} = xe^{-x} - 2e^{-x}$

When $x = 1$, $f''(x) = 1 \times e^{-1} - 2e^{-1} = -e^{-1}$. So $f''(x) < 0 \Rightarrow$ maximum

<u>The turning point is at $(1, e^{-1})$ and it is a maximum</u>

Note that we could have given the y coordinate as $1/e$ or as $0.368...$

Graphical behaviour of functions

Although you will often use your calculator to graph more complex functions, you must understand the relationship between various aspects of the function and its graph.

Vertical asymptotes: The function $f(x) = \dfrac{1}{x-4}$ is undefined when $x = 4$. This creates a "barrier" within the graph which is the line $x = 4$, and the graph gets ever closer to it without

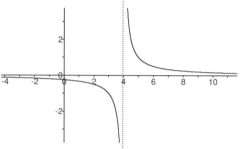

touching it – the definition of an *asymptote*. The graph usually climbs up towards $+\infty$ or drops towards $-\infty$ either side of the line. This will happen for *any* values of x which give a 0 on the denominator of the function.

Other asymptotes: It is useful to know what happens for very large values of $|x|$, ie at each end of the graph. Many graphs tend towards a *horizontal asymptote*, getting closer and closer to a line $y = k$. Consider the

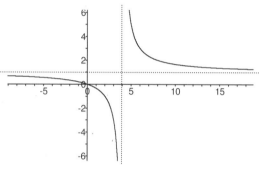

function $f(x) = \dfrac{x}{x-4}$. As the x values increase, the 4 on the denominator becomes insignificant. So the function tends towards $\dfrac{x}{x} = 1$. Another way to see this is to put in a large value of x. eg: $f(1000) = 1.004$.

Note that it is perfectly possible for a graph to cross a *horizontal* asymptote – it is not a barrier. Note also that an asymptote does not have to be horizontal – graphs can close in on *any* line. See the second example on the next page.

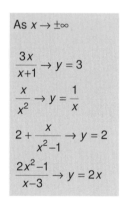

As $x \to \pm\infty$

$\dfrac{3x}{x+1} \to y = 3$

$\dfrac{x}{x^2} \to y = \dfrac{1}{x}$

$2 + \dfrac{x}{x^2-1} \to y = 2$

$\dfrac{2x^2-1}{x-3} \to y = 2x$

A few examples are shown on the left.

Sketching graphs: Follow these steps for drawing a "sketch" (as opposed to a "plot") of the graph of a complex function.

- Draw a pair of axes and put on any vertical asymptotes.
- Work out where the graph crosses the x- and y- axes by putting $y = 0$ and $x = 0$ (as long as the calculations are not too awkward). When you draw your sketch, ensure that the graph does not cross the axes at any other points.
- Draw in the asymptote toward which the graph tends.
- If required, put in further information concerning turning points and points of inflexion.
- Sketch the graph. In most cases, you will find that there is only one possible line which fits all the information you have already put in. If not, you may have to work out one or two points to fix the graph in position.

You will be expected to do this in conjunction with calculator graphical techniques. It is particularly important on the calculator to choose the correct "window" otherwise you can miss important detail.

Sketching Graphs – Examples

Sketch the graph of $f(x) = 1 - \dfrac{2x}{1+x^2}$ **including the coordinates of any turning points.**

- Vertical asymptote when $1 + x^2 = 0$, but this gives $x^2 = -1$. So, no values of x work, and therefore no asymptote.
- When $x = 0$, $y = 1$
- When $y = 0$, $0 = 1 - \dfrac{2x}{1+x^2}$. This is a quadratic equation which is solved on the right to give $x = 1$.
- Horizontal asymptote is $y = 1$ (try $x = 1000$)

So far, this information can be drawn on a pair of axes to give:

ow we need to differentiate and will use the quotient rule for the fractional part of the function.

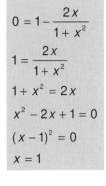

$$0 = 1 - \frac{2x}{1+x^2}$$
$$1 = \frac{2x}{1+x^2}$$
$$1 + x^2 = 2x$$
$$x^2 - 2x + 1 = 0$$
$$(x-1)^2 = 0$$
$$x = 1$$

$u = 2x, \qquad \dfrac{du}{dx} = 2$

$v = 1 + x^2, \qquad \dfrac{dv}{dx} = 2x$

$f'(x) = 0 - \dfrac{(1+x^2) \times 2 - 2x \times 2x}{(1+x^2)^2} = -\dfrac{2 - 2x^2}{(1+x^2)^2}$

For a fraction to equal 0, only the top line must be 0.

- For a turning point, $f'(x) = 0$, so $2 - 2x^2 = 0 \Rightarrow x = \pm 1$

We need the y-coordinates: Stationary points are $(1, 0)$ and $(-1, 2)$. Now the only possible graph which fits all the information is:

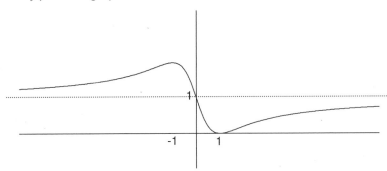

Sketch the graph of $y = \dfrac{x^2 - 1}{x - 2}$

- Vertical asymptote when $x = 2$
- When $x = 0$, $y = 0.5$
- When $y = 0$, $x = \pm 1$ (just make the top line 0)
- As $x \to \infty$, $y \to x + 2$ (ie The line $y = x + 2$ is an asymptote)

So far, we have enough to draw the diagram on the right. The graph will start down on the bottom left, close to $y = x$. It must then go through the three axis intercepts, before approaching the vertical asymptote. With no axis intercepts on the right hand side of $x = 2$, the only place for it is up in the little angle at the top. Perhaps a sketch is easier to appreciate!

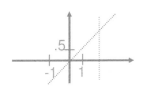

$$\frac{x^2 - 1}{x - 2} = \frac{x(x-2) + (2x-1)}{x-2}$$
$$= x + \frac{2x-1}{x-2}$$
As $x \to \infty$, $f(x) \to x+2$

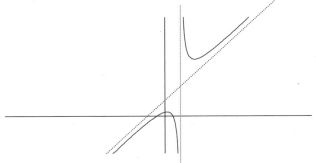

Applications of Differentiation

Equations of tangents: A tangent to a graph has the same gradient as at the point on the graph where the tangent touches. Knowing this, and the point itself, we can find the equation of the tangent. Remember that when you differentiate a function you get the *gradient function*.

---

eg: Find the equation of the tangent to y = 2x² – 4x + 3 at the point where x = 2.

- $\frac{dy}{dx} = 4x - 4$, so when x = 2, gradient = 4
- When x = 2, y = 3
- Equation is given by y – y₁ = m(x – x₁), so y – 3 = 4(x – 2)
  Equation of the tangent is y = 4x – 5

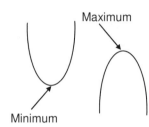

Maximum

Minimum

Maximum and minimum points: The point where a graph "turns round" can be very significant. For example, if the graph shows values of profit against selling price for a particular product, the maximum shows the selling price which leads to maximum profit.

- To find a maximum or minimum, differentiate the function then find where the gradient is 0.
- To tell which sort of point you have, use the second derivative or a sign diagram.
- Note that you do not need the graph in front of you to find the turning points. ▣ However, make sure you can use your calculator to find maximum and minimum values (for example, *find the x-coordinates of all maximums and minimums on the graph of f(x) = sin(1 + sinx), 0 ≤ x ≤ 6*)

Find the turning point on the graph of $y = \ln(2 + x^2)$, giving coordinates as exact values, and determine whether it is a maximum or minimum.

- $\frac{dy}{dx} = \frac{2x}{2 + x^2}$ (using the chain rule)

- For a turning point, $\frac{dy}{dx} = 0 \Rightarrow 2x = 0 \Rightarrow x = 0$

- So the turning point is at **(0, ln2)**

x	-1	0	1
dy/dx	-2/3	0	2/3
	\	—	/

The sign diagram shows the values of $\frac{dy}{dx}$ either side of the turning point. Drawing the gradients is not necessary, but it helps. I chose to use a sign diagram because the second derivative looked rather awkward.

- So (0, ln2) is a **minimum**   *(Check by drawing the graph)*

Velocity and acceleration: Since velocity is rate of change of distance, differentiating a distance-time function will give velocity. Similarly, differentiating a velocity-time function will give acceleration (which is the rate at which velocity changes).

YOU SOLVE

A ball is thrown in the air and its height in metres t seconds afterwards is given by the formula h = 20t - 5t². Find when the ball reaches its maximum height, and what this height is.

2s, 20m

Find the x coordinate of the point of inflexion closest to the origin on the graph of:
$y = x^2e^x$.
Differentiate (which rule?) twice and find where the second derivative = 0. You will need to factorise. Check it is a point of inflexion by inspecting points either side.

$$-2 + \sqrt{2}$$

A rectangle is bounded by the positive x-axis and the positive y-axis and the curve with equation $y = \dfrac{4-2x}{x+1}$. **Show that the rectangle has maximum area when its length is** $\sqrt{3} - 1$, **and find this area, giving your answer to 3 decimal places.**

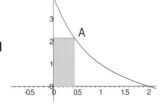

For all points A, the area of the rectangle will be the x coordinate multiplied by the y coordinate. We can then differentiate this expression and set it equal to 0 to find its maximum value.

$$A = \frac{4x - 2x^2}{x+1} \Rightarrow \frac{dA}{dx} = \frac{(x+1)(4-4x)-(4x-2x^2)}{(x+1)^2} \quad \text{(quotient rule)}$$

For this to be 0, the top line must be 0, and this reduces to the quadratic equation $x^2 + 2x - 2 = 0$. The only solution of this between 0 and 2 is $\sqrt{3} - 1$ (from the formula).

To test if it is a maximum, we look at the gradients either side. f'(0) = 4, f'(1) = -0.5, giving a maximum. Substituting into the formula for A, we find the maximum area is **1.072**

Related rates of change: Differentiating a function tells us how fast one variable is changing compared to another. Using the chain rule, we can compare how *three* inter-related variables are changing. Typically, a formula connects two of them. A question might look like this:

A circular oil slick is growing such that its radius is increasing at a constant rate of 5m/hour. How fast is the area increasing when the radius is 30m?

We want the rate of increase of area, ie $\dfrac{dA}{dt}$. Using the chain rule, and

the third variable (ie r), we get: $\dfrac{dA}{dt} = \dfrac{dA}{dr} \times \dfrac{dr}{dt}$ (note how dr "cancels").

We want $\dfrac{dA}{dt}$, we know $\dfrac{dr}{dt}$ so what about $\dfrac{dA}{dr}$? The connection between

A and r is that $A = \pi r^2$, so $\dfrac{dA}{dr} = 2\pi r$. Putting this together, we get:

$\dfrac{dA}{dt} = 2\pi r \times 5 = 2\pi \times 30 \times 5 = 300\pi$. So rate of increase of area = **942m²h⁻¹**

A tap leaks water at 2cm³/s into a cone, held vertex downwards. The cone has a radius of 12cm and a height of 18cm. Find the rate of rise of water level when the depth is 6cm.
Variables V, t and h (depth of water). You will need a general formula for the volume of water. Remember that $\dfrac{dh}{dV}$ is the reciprocal of $\dfrac{dV}{dh}$.

$$\frac{\pi}{8} \text{ cm/s}$$

Implicit Differentiation

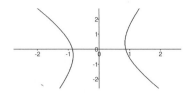

Implicit relations: A relation such as $y = 2x^2 - 3$ is called *explicit* because putting in any value of x immediately gives you a value of y. When x and y are mixed up, the relation is then called *implicit*: for example, $4x^2 + xy - y^2 = 3$ is an implicit relation. It may be possible to make x or y the subject, but not necessarily. Implicit relations are not usually functions (the graph of the relation above is on the left), but we can still find the gradient of the curve at all points (except where the tangent is vertical). Implicit differentiation gives us a way of finding the gradient at any point on the curve.

It is a common mistake to leave the constant on the RHS. But 3 differentiated is 0.

Implicit differentiation: When you differentiate a function *with respect to x* this means that you are calculating how fast the function is changing compared to how fast x is changing. With implicit differentiation, we differentiate *each term* of the relation with respect to x. If it's already a function of x, no problem. If it's a function of y, differentiate it with respect to y then multiply by $\frac{dy}{dx}$; in other words, we find out how fast it is changing compared to y then multiply that by the rate of change of y compared to x. It sounds a bit complicated, but what it comes down to is that a term such as y^2, when differentiated with respect to x, becomes $2y\frac{dy}{dx}$. Differentiating all the terms in the relation above, and noting that xy will have to be differentiated using the product rule, we get this:

$$8x + x\frac{dy}{dx} + y - 2y\frac{dy}{dx} = 0$$

What do we do with it now? That depends on the question:

- Find the gradient at the point $\left(\frac{\sqrt{3}}{2}, 0\right)$. Substituting the coordinates gives $8\frac{\sqrt{3}}{2} + \frac{\sqrt{3}}{2}\frac{dy}{dx} = 0 \Rightarrow \frac{dy}{dx} = -8$

- Find $\frac{dy}{dx}$ in terms of y and x. To do this, we make $\frac{dy}{dx}$ the subject, just as if it were an ordinary algebraic variable. Check that this gives $\frac{dy}{dx} = \frac{-8x-y}{x-2y} = \frac{8x+y}{2y-x}$.

Remember that implicit differentiation is just another weapon in the differentiation armoury. Having differentiated, you can tackle all the standard types of question such as finding the equations of tangents, finding turning points and so on.

YOU SOLVE

Find the equation of the normal to the curve $2x^2 + 4y^2 = 6$ at the point where $x = 1$ and y is negative.

$y = -2x + 1$

Indefinite Integration

Integration is sometimes called "anti-differentiation": that is, it is the reverse operation to integration. However, the notation is very different, and you must understand two forms – the indefinite and the definite integral.

Notation: If we just consider functions of the form ax^n then, to reverse the differentiation process, we must add 1 to n then divide by the new power. For example, $4x^2$ integrated is $\dfrac{4x^3}{3}$. The full notation for this is: $\int 4x^2 dx = \dfrac{4x^3}{3}$. The $\int$ sign means "integrate", then you put the function you want to integrate, then you put dx. However, the answer is not entirely correct. If you differentiate $\dfrac{4x^3}{3}$ you will certainly get $4x^2$, but this will also be true if you differentiate $\dfrac{4x^3}{3} + 2$, $\dfrac{4x^3}{3} - 1$, and so on. In other words, when we integrate, there could be a constant at the end. Since we don't know what it is, we add a c which is called "the constant of integration." So, $\int 4x^2 dx = \dfrac{4x^3}{3} + c$, and you add the c to every indefinite integral – hence the word "indefinite."

> You will actually make use of the dx in integration by substitution and differential equations. Otherwise, think of it as a decorative – but necessary – piece of notation.

Integrating x^n: Generally, $\int ax^n dx = \dfrac{ax^{n+1}}{n+1} + c$ and, as with differentiation, $n \in \mathbb{Q}$. There is one exception, and that is when integrating $1/x$. Since this is x^{-1}, the rule above would give $x^0/0$ and this is undefined. But when we differentiate $\ln x$ we get $1/x$, so it follows that $\int \dfrac{1}{x} dx = \ln|x| + c$

Integrating other functions:

$f(x)$	$\int f(x) dx$
$\sin x$	$-\cos x$
$\cos x$	$\sin x$
e^x	e^x

Also, as with differentiation, it is true that
$$\int f(x) + g(x) dx = \int f(x) + \int g(x) \text{ and } \int kf(x) dx = k \int f(x) dx$$

Integrating f(ax + b): By reversing the chain rule it can be shown that:

$$\int f(ax+b) dx = \frac{1}{a} F(ax+b) + c, \text{ where F is f integrated.}$$

Examples: $\int (3x+4)^3 dx = \dfrac{1}{3} \times \dfrac{(3x+4)^4}{4} = \dfrac{(3x+4)^4}{12} + c$

$\int \cos(2x-5) dx = \dfrac{1}{2} \sin(2x-5) + c$

$\int (5x+1)^{\frac{1}{2}} dx = \dfrac{1}{5} \times \dfrac{(5x+1)^{\frac{3}{2}}}{\frac{3}{2}} = \dfrac{2(5x+1)^{\frac{3}{2}}}{15} + c$

$\int e^{(2x)} dx = \dfrac{1}{2} e^{(2x)} + c$

Find: a) $\dfrac{d}{dx}(1-2x)^3$

The $\dfrac{d}{dx}$ symbol is a shorthand for "differentiate." Because the function is composite, we must use the chain rule. The "inner function" is 1 - 2x which differentiates to -2. So:

$$\dfrac{d}{dx}(1-2x)^3 = -2\times 3(1-2x)^2 = \underline{-6(1-2x)^2}$$

   b) $\int(1-2x)^3\,dx$

This is an integral of the form f(ax + b) so, using the formula, we get:

$$\int(1-2x)^3\,dx = \dfrac{1}{-2}\times\dfrac{(1-2x)^4}{4}+c = \underline{-\dfrac{(1-2x)^4}{8}+c}$$

Solving gradient function equations: In some questions we are given the *gradient* (ie derived) function and asked to find the original function which gave rise to it. This means we must integrate the gradient function. For example, if $f'(x) = 3x^2 - x^3$ find f(x).

So, $f(x) = \int 3x^2 - x^3\,dx = x^3 - \frac{1}{4}x^4 + c$, but we will need more information to find the value of c. Suppose we know that f(2) = 6 (in other words, when x = 2, y = 6). If we substitute this into the equation we get: 6 = 8 − 4 + c, and c = 2. So the function we are looking for is $f(x) = x^3 - \frac{1}{4}x^4 + 2$.

Let f′(x) = 1 − x^2. Given that f(3) = 0, find f(x).

First integrate f′(x) to get $f(x) = x - \dfrac{x^3}{3}+c$. Now substitute x = 3 and f(x) = 0 to get

$$0 = 3 - \dfrac{3^3}{3}+c \Rightarrow c = 6. \text{ So, } f(x) = x - \dfrac{x^3}{3}+6.$$

YOU SOLVE

If f′(x) = cosx and f(π/2) = -2, find f(x).

$\underline{f(x) = \sin x - 3}$

YOU SOLVE

A curve with equation y = f(x) passes through the point (1, 3). Its gradient function is f′(x) = -4x + 2. Find the equation of the curve.

$\underline{f(x) = -2x^2 + 2x + 3}$

Definite Integration

Area under a curve: The gradient at a point on a distance-time curve gives us velocity. The *area* under a velocity-time curve gives us distance travelled, so we can consider finding the area under the curve as a sort of inverse function to calculating the gradient. It therefore follows that integration will give us the area under a curve, but we need to also give the boundaries of the area. These boundaries are called *limits* and, when applied to an integral, turn an indefinite integral into a definite one.

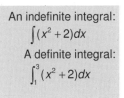

An indefinite integral:
$$\int (x^2 + 2)dx$$
A definite integral:
$$\int_1^3 (x^2 + 2)dx$$

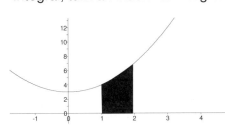

The graph shows the function $f(x) = x^2 + 3$. The shaded area is between the *x*-values of 1 and 2, and is denoted by the *definite* integral $\int_1^2 (x^2 + 3)dx$

The procedure for calculating the area is as follows:

- Integrate the function, omitting the constant of integration.
- Put the result in square brackets with the limits outside.
- Substitute the limits into the integrated function (upper limit first) and subtract the two numbers – this gives the area.

The *c* can be left out because it will always cancel out in the subtraction which follows.

In the example above, the procedure looks like this:

$$\int_1^2 (x^2 + 3)dx = \left[\frac{x^3}{3} + 3x \right]_1^2$$

$$= \left(\frac{2^3}{3} + 3 \times 2 \right) - \left(\frac{1^3}{3} + 3 \times 1 \right)$$

$$= \left(\frac{8}{3} + 6 \right) - \left(\frac{1}{3} + 3 \right) = 5\tfrac{1}{3}$$

Substitute the limits without any calculations at first, then work through carefully. Beware minus signs!

Make sure you know how to use your calculator to work out definite integrals.

The square brackets have the meaning "substitute the limits then subtract".

Sometimes we need to find the area between the curve and the *y*-axis. The working is the same, except that we must first write the function in terms of *y*.

The diagram shows the graph of the function $y = 1 + 1/x$. Find the *exact* value of the area of the shaded region from $y = 4/3$ to $y = 2$.

First the function must be rearranged to become $x = 1/(y - 1)$. Now we can work out the integral. Note we must give the *exact* value – so a calculator result is no good.

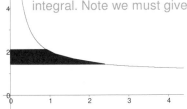

$$\int_{\frac{4}{3}}^2 \frac{1}{y-1} dy = \left[\ln(y-1) \right]_{\frac{4}{3}}^2$$

$$= (\ln(2-1)) - (\ln(\tfrac{4}{3} - 1))$$

$$= \ln 1 - \ln \tfrac{1}{3} = \ln 3$$

<u>Area = ln3</u>

The diagram shows part of the curve of $y = 12x^2(1 - x)$. Write down an integral which represents the area cut off by the curve and the *x*-axis, and find this area.

You will first need to find where the graph cuts the x-axis. And don't forget to multiply out before integrating.

$$\int_0^1 12x^2(1 - x)dx, \quad \text{Area} = 1$$

YOU SOLVE

Integration By Substitution

Substituting a single letter for part of a function can make an apparently unintegrable function possible. It is important that all traces of the original letter are "removed". Suppose you are going to replace a function of x with a function of u; the following steps must be taken:

- Choose the substitution (often given to you)
- Work out $\dfrac{du}{dx}$ and hence the substitution for dx
- Look ahead to see if anything will cancel when you substitute
- Do the substitution, including the limits (if there are any)
- Simplify if possible, putting multiplying or dividing constants outside
- INTEGRATE (this stage is sometimes forgotten)!
- Resubstitute x if the integral was indefinite.

Watch these stages in action in the following examples:

Integrate $x^3(x^2 - 2)^4$

$$\int x^3(x^2 - 2)^4\, dx$$

$$= \int x^3 u^4 \frac{du}{2x}$$

$$= \tfrac{1}{2}\int x^2 u^4\, du$$

$$= \tfrac{1}{2}\int (u+2)u^4\, du$$

- Substitute $u = x^2 - 2$
- $\dfrac{du}{dx} = 2x \Rightarrow dx = \dfrac{du}{2x}$
- The $2x$ on the bottom will cancel with the x^3

Now we can multiply out and integrate to get:

$$\frac{1}{2}\left(\frac{u^6}{6} + \frac{2u^5}{5}\right) + c \text{ which resubstitutes to } \frac{(x^2 - 2)^6}{12} + \frac{(x^2 - 2)^5}{5} + c.$$

The next example involves a bottom line and limits. Note how simple algebra is used to split the integral into two fractions.

Integrate $\displaystyle\int_0^5 \frac{x}{\sqrt{x+4}}\, dx$

$$= \int_4^9 \frac{u - 4}{\sqrt{u}}\, du$$

$$= \int_4^9 \left(\frac{u}{\sqrt{u}} - \frac{4}{\sqrt{u}}\right) du$$

$$= \int_4^9 (u^{\frac{1}{2}} - 4u^{-\frac{1}{2}})\, du$$

- Substitute $u = x + 4$
- $\dfrac{du}{dx} = 1 \Rightarrow dx = du$
- When $x = 0$, $u = 4$
- When $x = 5$, $u = 9$
- We also need to use the fact that $x = u - 4$

You should be able to work this through to get **4.667**

An important class of substitutions are those of type $\displaystyle\int \frac{1}{a^2 + x^2}\, dx$ and $\displaystyle\int \frac{1}{\sqrt{a^2 - x^2}}\, dx$. Here, we substitute $x = f(u)$: in the first one, $x = a\tan u$; in the second, $x = a\sin u$.

Integrate $\displaystyle\int \frac{1}{4 + x^2}$

$$= \int \frac{1}{4 + 4\tan^2 u}\, 2\sec^2 u\, du$$

$$= \int \frac{1}{4(1 + \tan^2 u)}\, 2\sec^2 u\, du$$

$$= \int \frac{1}{2}\, du$$

$$= \frac{1}{2}u + c = \frac{1}{2}\tan^{-1} x + c$$

- Substitute $x = 2\tan u$
- $\dfrac{dx}{du} = 2\sec^2 u \Rightarrow dx = 2\sec^2 u\, du$
- We need $1 + \tan^2 u = \sec^2 u$

Integration by Parts

The typical scenario for integration by parts is when you have two functions (often of different types) multiplied together. If the two functions are called u and $\dfrac{dv}{dx}$, then the formula looks like this:

The second function is called $\dfrac{dv}{dx}$ because it is going to be integrated, giving v. This makes the formula simpler to understand!

$\displaystyle\int u\dfrac{dv}{dx}dx = uv - \int v\dfrac{du}{dx}dx$. It's easier, perhaps in words: one of the two functions (u) *only* gets differentiated in the formula, the other *only* gets integrated. It may help to think pictorially:

To integrate $3xe^{2x}$, for example, we first need to decide which function is better integrated, which differentiated. Clearly e^{2x} is better to integrate since it doesn't "get more complicated", and $3x$ is better to differentiate because it gets simpler. So, choose $u = 3x$ and $\dfrac{dv}{dx} = e^{2x}$ which means that $\dfrac{du}{dx} = 3$ and $v = \tfrac{1}{2}e^{2x}$, so:

$$\int 3xe^{2x}dx = 3x \times \tfrac{1}{2}e^{2x} - \int 3 \times \tfrac{1}{2}e^{2x}dx = \tfrac{3}{2}xe^{2x} - \tfrac{3}{4}e^{2x} + c$$

A simpler, informal version of the formula is $\int fg' = fg - \int g'f$

If there are limits, it is easier to leave them right to the end, then substitute them.

Repeated integration by parts: Once you have worked your way through the formula, you still have an integral to do, and this could be any function, any method. Sometimes it is another integration by parts, as in this example:

Integrate $x^2\cos x$.

Here, we choose $u = x^2$ and $\dfrac{dv}{dx} = \cos x$. So $\dfrac{du}{dx} = 2x$ and $v = \sin x$.

Substituting into the formula gives $\int x^2 \cos x\, dx = x^2 \sin x - \int 2x\sin x\, dx$.

But the second integral must itself be done by parts, and it is important to keep it in a bracket because of the minus sign outside. Work this through to get $x^2\sin x - (-2x\cos x + 2\sin x) = x^2\sin x + 2x\cos x - 2\sin x$.

Inx: Because you cannot directly integrate $\ln x$, and also because it differentiates easily to $\dfrac{1}{x}$, put $u = \ln x$ when it appears in an integration by parts.

Integrate $\ln x\sqrt{x}$.

Remember that $\dfrac{x^a}{x^b} = x^{a-b}$. You will need this in the integral.

$\tfrac{2}{3}x^{\frac{3}{2}}\ln x - \tfrac{4}{9}x^{\frac{3}{2}} + c$

YOU SOLVE

General Methods for Integration

You may find that you can do all the various integration methods when you are told which one to use but, faced with an integration in a test or exam, it seems there are a million different ways of tackling it. This section doesn't have all the answers, but it provides some pointers for you in the form of questions you should ask yourself.

Integrals with no denominator:

Note that if any integral has a multiplying or dividing constant in front of the function, it just sits there while you integrate the function part.

- Is it a simple "reverse differentiation?"
  Examples: $\cos x$, $3x^2 - 2x + 1$, $(x-3)^2$, $\sec^2 x$
- Is it of the form $f(ax + b)$? The answer will be $\frac{1}{a}F(ax + b)$
  Examples: $\sin(2x - 3)$, $(3x - 4)^5$, e^{4-x}, $\sqrt{(4x + 1)}$
- Might the trigonometric formulae be useful?
  Examples: $\sin^2 x$, $4\cos x \sin x$, $\tan^2 x$
- Is it two different types of function multiplied together? If so, use integration by parts.
  Examples: xe^{2x}, $x^2 \sin x$, $\ln x (= 1 \times \ln x)$
- If none of the above work, try integration by substitution. (In some cases you will be able to reverse the chain rule, but only do this if you really know what you are doing – these are marked with a * in the examples)
  Examples: $x(2x - 3)^6$, $x\sin(x^2 - 3)^*$, $\sin x \cos^2 x^*$, $x^3\sqrt{(x^2 - 4)}$

Integrals with a denominator:
The number of possibilities expands for two main reasons. Firstly, there are plenty of opportunities for algebraic manipulation. Secondly, there is the whole class of integrals resulting in logs.

- Is the denominator to the power 1, and is the numerator the derivative of the denominator (or a simple multiple). If so, try ln(denominator).
  Examples: $\dfrac{2}{x-3}$, $\dfrac{x}{x^2 +1}$, $\dfrac{\sin x}{\cos x}$, $\dfrac{e^x}{e^x +1}$

  Don't forget to check whether you need to multiply by an appropriate constant at the end.
- Check for simple algebraic manipulation. For example, splitting up into several fractions, dividing the denominator into the numerator.
  Examples: $\dfrac{x^2 - 2x + 1}{x}$, $\dfrac{2x + 3}{x-1}$ $\left(= 2 + \dfrac{5}{x-1}\right)$
- Don't forget the standard integrals, particularly the inverse trigonometric functions.
  Examples: $\dfrac{3}{x^2 +1}$, $\dfrac{2}{\sqrt{1 - x^2}}$
- If all the above fail, rewrite the denominator in the numerator with a negative power, and see if inspection or reverse chain rule work.
  Examples: $\dfrac{2}{(x-1)^2}$, $\dfrac{2x}{\sqrt{x^2 +1}}$, $\dfrac{4}{e^x}$, $\dfrac{\cos x}{\sin^3 x}$
- As a last resort, perhaps, try substitution.
  Examples: $\dfrac{x}{\sqrt{x-1}}$,

On the next page there are plenty of integrals for you to try – work through the above checklist if you need to.

Integration Practice

On this page there is a variety of integrals for you to try in the top block. The middle block contains hints in case you get stuck, and all the solutions are at the bottom. The practice integrals contain many that have been set in papers over the last few years.

1. $\int \dfrac{4x}{1+x^2}\,dx$ 2. $\int \dfrac{x}{x+10}\,dx$ 3. $\int 4x(3x-5)dx$ 4. $\int \dfrac{10}{x^2+25}\,dx$

5. $\int \tan^2 x\,dx$ 6. $\int t\sin(\frac{\pi}{3}t)dt$ 7. $\int x\sqrt{2x+3}\,dx$ 8. $\int x\sqrt{x^2-1}\,dx$

9. $\int \cos^2 x\,dx$ 10. $\int \dfrac{1+x}{\sqrt{1-x^2}}\,dx$ 11. $\int 2t\sin(t^2)dt$ 12. $\int \dfrac{1+\cos x}{\sin x + x}\,dx$

13. $\int \tan 3x\,dx$ 14. $\int \ln x\,dx$ 15. $\int x^2 e^x\,dx$ 16. $\int \dfrac{x^3}{\sqrt{1-x^2}}\,dx$

---

1. Top is a multiple of the bottom differentiated. Try ln(bottom line); adjust the constant.
2. Substitution, or divide the denominator into the numerator.
3. Just multiply out, then integrate
4. Standard integral – look it up in your formulae.
5. Which trigonometric identity contains $\tan^2 x$?
6. Product of two different types of function – by parts.
7. The outside is not the derivative of the inside; you can't multiply out; must be substitution. Try $u = 2x + 3$.
8. Outside is a multiple of the inside differentiated so you can use the reverse chain rule. You can also substitute.
9. Trig. formulae. Look at the formula for cos2x.
10. Looks complicated – can we simplify algebraically? Split the numerator so you get two fractions; the first is a standard integral, for the second, write the denominator as a negative power in the numerator.
11. Looks like parts – but wait: the outside is the inside differentiated, so we can use the reverse chain rule. Try differentiating $\cos(t^2)$ and see what you get.
12. What is the connection between numerator and denominator?
13. Use the formula connecting sin, cos and tan.
14. A sneaky one. Write as $1 \times \ln x$, and use parts.
15. Parts – but you will need to do it twice.
16. Try substitution.

$2\ln(1+x^2)+c$; $x-10\ln|x+10|+c$; $4x^3-10x^2+c$; $2\tan^{-1}(\frac{x}{5})+c$;

$\tan x - x + c$; $-\frac{3}{\pi}t\cos(\frac{\pi}{3}t)+\frac{9}{\pi^2}\sin(\frac{\pi}{3}t)+c$;

$\frac{1}{10}(2x+3)^{\frac{5}{2}}-\frac{1}{2}(2x+3)^{\frac{3}{2}}+c=\frac{1}{5}(x-1)(2x+3)^{\frac{3}{2}}+c$; $\frac{1}{3}(x^2-1)^{\frac{3}{2}}+c$;

$\frac{1}{4}\sin 2x+\frac{1}{2}x+c$; $\sin^{-1}x-\sqrt{1-x^2}+c$; $-\cos t^2 + c$;

$\ln|x+\sin x|+c$; $-\frac{1}{3}\ln|\cos 3x|+c=\frac{1}{3}\ln|\sec 3x|+c$;

$x\ln|x|-x+c$; $x^2 e^x - 2xe^x + 2e^x + c$; $-(1-x^2)^{\frac{1}{2}}+\frac{1}{3}(1-x^2)^{\frac{3}{2}}+c$

Note how in some of the examples, the job isn't finished when the integration has been done. You may well have to perform further algebraic manipulation (eg: 7).

Differential Equations

$\frac{dy}{dx}$ is called a *differential* and any equation containing one is a *differential equation*. We can solve an equation of the form $\frac{dy}{dx} = f(x)$ by integrating both sides wrtx (with respect to x) leading to the solution $y = F(x)$. For example, $\frac{dy}{dx} = 3x^2 + 1$ integrates to give the solution $y = x^3 + x + c$. This is called the *general solution*. If we have been given a point on the solution curve, (1, 3) for example, we can substitute that to get c. This leads to the *particular solution* which in this case is $y = x^3 + x + 1$. There are two other types of differential equation to grapple with:

- $\frac{dy}{dx} = g(y)$. The problem here is that you cannot integrate the RHS wrtx because the letter is wrong. A little fiddle sorts this out: take $g(y)$ over to the LHS, and bring dx up to the RHS. For example:

$$\frac{dy}{dx} = e^y \Rightarrow \frac{dy}{e^y} = dx$$

$$\int \frac{1}{e^y} dy = \int 1 dx \Rightarrow -e^{-y} = x + c$$

> The variables may not be x and y, but it doesn't matter. The important thing is to make sure letters are not mixed up together when you integrate.

- $\frac{dy}{dx} = f(x)g(y)$. In this case, we still take the $g(y)$ down and bring the dx up, and then the $f(x)$ can team up with the dx. This will only work if the variables can be separated, and it may be necessary to do some algebra first. For example:

$$\frac{dy}{dx} = 2xy^2 + 2x \Rightarrow \frac{dy}{dx} = 2x(y^2 + 1)$$

$$\int \frac{1}{y^2 + 1} dy = \int 2x dx$$

$$\tan^{-1} y = x^2 + c$$

You must be prepared to use *any* of the integral techniques you have learnt when solving differential equations.

Solve the differential equation $\frac{x}{x-2} \frac{dy}{dx} + 1 = y$ **given that** $y = 2$ **when** $x = 3$.

The key here is to rearrange the equation so that x appears only on the RHS, and y on the LHS.

We get $\frac{1}{y-1} dy = \frac{x-2}{x} dx$. Then, $\int \frac{1}{y-1} dy = \int 1 - \frac{2}{x} dx$ and hence $\ln(y - 1) = x - 2\ln x + c$.

Substituting the values of x and y gives $c = 2\ln 3 - 3$. Should the question ask you to write the answer in the form $y = ...$, you need to re-arrange before substituting. See if you can get to the simplest form which is $y = \frac{Ae^x}{x^2} + 1$, and hence $A = 9e^{-3}$. *(Hint: $2\ln x = \ln x^2$)*

YOU SOLVE

Find the general solution of the differential equation $\frac{1}{x} \frac{dy}{dx} = \frac{\ln x}{\sin y}$.

$$-\cos y = \frac{x^2}{2} \ln x - \frac{x^2}{4} + c$$

Applications: A differential is a rate of increase or decrease, and this is always the starting point for practical applications. Suppose, for example, that a town's rate of population increase is proportional to the population; this leads to the equation $\dfrac{dP}{dt} = kP$. To solve this, we divide by P, and continue

as follows: $\int \dfrac{1}{P} dP = \int k\, dt \Rightarrow \ln P = kt + c$. In this sort of situation it

is normal to make P the subject: $P = e^{kt + c}$ or $P = Ae^{kt}$. With two constants two find, we need two pieces of information. Suppose we are given that that $t = 0$ represents the year 1990 and the population was then 3000. We are also told that in 2000, the population was 3500.

Then: $2000 = Ae^0 \Rightarrow A = 2000$

$3500 = 2000 \times e^{10k} \Rightarrow 1.75 = e^{10k} \Rightarrow k = 0.0560$

Thus, the full solution is $P = 2000e^{0.0560t}$.

> We can use the solution to solve further questions such as "what will the population be in 2005?" or "when will the population reach 10000?"
> *Answers: 4632 and 2019.*

Speed and acceleration are other typical quantities that form the basis of differential equations.

> Velocity $= \dfrac{ds}{dt}$
>
> Acceleration $= \dfrac{dv}{dt}$

The velocity of an object, v, at time t is given by $v = 3e^{-t/2}$. Find how far it travels from $t = 0$ until $t = 2$.

$\dfrac{ds}{dt} = 3e^{-\frac{1}{2}t} \Rightarrow \int ds = \int 3e^{-\frac{1}{2}t} dt$ so $s = -6e^{-\frac{1}{2}t} + c$

When $t = 0$, $s = -6 + c$. When $t = 2$, $s = -2.21 + c$. Thus the distance travelled is $(-2.21 + c) - (-6 + c) = \underline{\textbf{3.79}}$

Often, questions are more algebraic.

The velocity of an object, v, at time t is given by $v = ke^{2t}$. Find the distance travelled between $t = 0$ and $t = T$.

Using similar working to the above example, we find that $s = 0.5ke^{2t} + c$.

When $t = 0$, $s = 0.5k + c$

When $t = T$, $s = 0.5ke^{2T} + c$

So, distance travelled $= (0.5ke^{2T} + c) - (0.5k + c) = \underline{\textbf{0.5k(e}^{2T}\textbf{-1)}}$

The formula for the acceleration of a hailstone is $a = 10 - 0.5v$, where v is its speed in ms^{-1}. By writing a as a differential, find a general formula for its speed in terms of the time, t, since its formation. Hence write down its terminal velocity.

YOU SOLVE

$v = 20 - Ae^{-\frac{1}{2}t}$, $20ms^{-1}$

A sample of radioactive material decays at a rate which is proportional to its mass, m. Given that 50g of material decays to 48g in 10 years, find the "half-life", ie the time taken for a given mass to halve.

You will need a minus sign on the right hand side of the differential equation because the rate of change is negative. You are given two facts (although it only looks like one), so you can find both the constant of proportionality and the constant of integration.

YOU SOLVE

$\underline{m = 50e^{-0.00408t}}$, $\underline{\text{170 years}}$

Volumes of Revolution

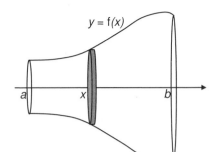

$y = f(x)$

a x b

dx is used for a very small distance in the x direction

On page 89 we saw how definite integration can be used to calculate the area under a curve. This can be extended to calculate the volume generated when part of a curve is rotated through 360º around either the x-axis or the y-axis. The diagram on the left shows the shape generated when the part of the curve of $y = f(x)$ lying between $x = a$ and $x = b$ is rotated around the x-axis. Imagine a cross-section of the shape at a distance x from the origin; it will be a disc. What is its volume?

- Its radius is f(x)
- So its cross-sectional area is $\pi\{f(x)\}^2$
- If its width is dx, its volume is $\pi\{f(x)\}^2 dx$

The overall volume will be the sum of an infinite number of such discs, and hence is found by integration.

- $V = \int \pi\{f(x)\}^2 dx$

For clarity, this is usually written as $V = \int \pi y^2 dx$

The area between the graph of $y = e^x$ and the x-axis from $x = 0$ to $x = k$ is rotated about the x-axis. Find, in terms of k, e and π, the volume generated.

Using the formula above, we get:

$V = \int_0^k \pi(e^x)^2 dx$

$= \pi \int_0^k e^{2x} dx$

$= \pi \left[\frac{1}{2} e^{2x} \right]_0^k$

$= \pi \left(\frac{1}{2} e^{2k} - \frac{1}{2} e^0 \right)$

$\frac{\pi(e^{2k} - 1)}{2}$

YOU SOLVE

The area between the curve $y = 2x - x^2$ and the line $y = x$ is rotated about the x-axis through 360º. Find the volume of the solid generated.

First find the points of intersection, then find the volume generated by the curve. The line will generate a cone: find its volume and subtract.

0.628

In some questions you are asked to rotate the area around the y-axis. In such cases you must rearrange the equation in terms of y, and then use $V = \int \pi y^2 dy$. For example, the area between the graph of $y = \sqrt{x+2}$ and the two axes is rotated through 360º about the y-axis. What is the volume generated? Rearranging, we get $x = y^2 - 2$. The graph intersects the y-axis at $(0, \sqrt{2})$, and the volume will be $\int_0^{\sqrt{2}} \pi(y^2 - 2)^2 dy$. Check this gives 33.2

Calculus – Non-Calculator Techniques

Differentiation: Continuing the thread of graph sketching (see page 82 onwards), you must be able to calculate the coordinates of turning points without the help of your calculator. But, further than this, you should be able to calculate maximum and minimum values in general.

Example: A right-angled triangle has the lengths of its two shorter sides as x and $3 - x$. Prove that the minimum length of the hypotenuse occurs when the triangle is isosceles.

Solution: The hypotenuse has length (using Pythagoras' Theorem) $\sqrt{x^2 + (3-x)^2} = \sqrt{2x^2 - 6x + 9}$. The minimum of this function occurs when $2x^2 - 6x + 9$ is also a minimum.

$\dfrac{d(2x^2 - 6x + 9)}{dx} = 4x - 6$, and hence there is a minimum when $4x - 6 = 0$, thus when $x = 1.5$. This means that both short sides have length 1.5, and the triangle is therefore isosceles.

When differentiating functions such as $\ln x$ and e^x and substituting values, you will need to give your answers as exact values.

Find the maximum and minimum values on the graph of $y = x^2 e^{-x}$, and also the equation of the tangent to the graph where $x = 1$.

First we need to differentiate the function, for which we use the product rule.

$$\frac{dy}{dx} = 2xe^{-x} - x^2 e^{-x} = xe^{-x}(2 - x)$$

This will equal 0 when $x = 0$ or 2 (e^x and e^{-x} can never be zero). Thus the turning points are at **(0, 0) and (2, $4e^{-2}$)**. By differentiating again you can find that the first of these is a minimum and the second a maximum.

When $x = 1$, the y-coordinate is e^{-1}, or $\dfrac{1}{e}$. Which form should you use? It depends on the question, so you should be prepared to be flexible. In this case, since we are going to find the equation of a line, we don't want powers of -1 getting in the way, so the second form will be better. The gradient is $\dfrac{2}{e} - \dfrac{1}{e} = \dfrac{1}{e}$.

$$y - y_1 = m(x - x_1)$$

$$y - \frac{1}{e} = \frac{1}{e}(x - 1)$$

$$ey - 1 = x - 1$$

Thus the equation of the tangent is **$ey = x$.**

Definite integrals: Many questions involving integrals are algebraic, or involve the substitution of letters rather than numbers, but you are probably used to carrying out straight definite integrals by using your GDC. Without the calculator, one of the main causes of error is minus signs: you will always have one, and often more. It pays not to take shortcuts, and to use brackets. Set out your working like this:

$$\int_{\frac{\pi}{2}}^{\pi} 3\sin x\, dx = \left[-3\cos x\right]_{\frac{\pi}{2}}^{\pi} = (-3\cos(\pi)) - (-3\cos(\tfrac{\pi}{2})) = (-3 \times -1) - (-3 \times 0)$$

Thus we get the definite integral as $3 - 0 = 3$.

Now work out these integrals without using a calculator:

$$\int_0^3 e^{-x}dx, \quad \int_3^4 \frac{x}{4-x^2}dx, \quad \int_{-1}^1 \left(\frac{1}{x^2} - x\right)dx, \quad \int_0^{\frac{\pi}{3}}(2 + 10\sin 5x)dx$$

YOU SOLVE

If $y = e^{-x}\cos x$ determine, in exact form, the three values of x between 0 and 3π for which $\dfrac{dy}{dx} = 0$. Show that the corresponding values of y form a geometric progression with common ratio $-e^{-\pi}$.

$\dfrac{3}{4}\pi, \dfrac{7}{4}\pi, \dfrac{11}{4}\pi$

YOU SOLVE

Find (without using a calculator) the value of x at which the function $f(x) = \dfrac{x+3}{\sqrt{(1+x^2)}}$ has a turning point, and determine whether it is a maximum or minimum.

$x = \frac{1}{3}$, max

MAXIMISING YOUR MARKS

Remember that the examiner is on your side – he *wants* to give you marks! Make it easy for him to find them, even if you are not quite sure what you are doing or if you are getting wrong answers. You cannot *lose* marks for doing things wrong. LEARN THIS CHECKLIST.

Before you start a question:
- Read it carefully so you know what it is about.
- Highlight important words.

Answering a question:
- Check any calculations you do, preferably using a different method or order of operation.
- Show your working – there are often marks for method as well as for the right answer. And, in a longer question, a wrong answer at the start may mean lots more wrong answers – but the examiner will probably give you marks for correct methods, and will check your working against your original answer.
- Make sure you have answered *exactly* what the question asked. For example, have you been asked to calculate the new value of an investment or the amount of interest earned.
- In longer questions, don't worry if you can't work out the answer to a part. Carry on with the rest, using their answer (if one is given) or even making up a reasonable answer.
- Don't spend too long on any question or part of a question – you may lose the opportunity to answer easier questions later on. You can always come back and fill in gaps.
- The algebra can be tough – keep going!
- Check the units in questions – are they mixed?

The "golden three":
- WHAT are you working out?
- HOW are you going to work it out?
- WHAT is the answer?

eg: Where do the lines
$y = x + 3$ and $x + 2y = 0$
intersect?

Lines intersect when $y = -2y + 3$
$$3y = 3$$
$$y = 1$$
Point of intersection = (-2, 1)

| WHAT | HOW | ANSWER |

Diagrams:
- Do not assume facts from diagrams, especially if they are marked NOT TO SCALE. For example, it may *look* like a right angle but does the question *tell* you that it is. Two lines may *look* parallel but they aren't unless you are *told* they are.
- And do draw your own diagrams – not necessarily to hand in as part of the question, but to help you sort out what's going on.

Key words in questions:
- STATE – put the answer down without working (should be an easy one)!
- WRITE DOWN – minimal working required.
- SHOW – show enough working to get to the given answer.
- EVALUATE – give a value to, work out.
- SKETCH A GRAPH – draw its shape and show key points (eg: where it cuts the axes)
- PLOT A GRAPH – work out points and draw the graph accurately
- EXACT VALUE – not a rounded decimal eg: 2π, not 6.28...

SHOW $x = 3$ is the solution of
$2x + 1 = 7$.
$$2 \times 3 + 1 = 7$$
(We have not had to *solve* the equation)

When you have answered the question:
- Check you have answered every part of the question.
- Check you have answered exactly what was asked.
- Check you have answered to the correct accuracy (normally 3 SF)
- Check that what you have written is clear, and that your answer is not mixed up in the working somewhere.

DO THESE CHECKS – you will probably pick up a few marks.

ASSESSMENT DETAILS

The three Higher Level papers count for 80% of your final mark, the remaining 20% being contributed by the internally assessed portfolio.

You should prepare yourself carefully for the exams, allowing for all eventualities. For example, make sure you have a spare set of batteries for your GDC, and that it only has legal programs in its memory. You should take at least two pens, and also pencils, ruler and eraser for drawing diagrams. You will be given a clean copy of the HL information booklet (you cannot take your own in); if you have not used it very much during lessons, part of your revision should involve getting to know the booklet well so that you can easily find relevant formulae and tables.

Papers 1 and 2 each consist of about 10 short response and about 5 extended response questions, the only difference being that you are allowed a GDC in Paper 2. Since the papers are 2 hours long, you should be aiming to answer one short question every 5 minutes and one long question every 10 minutes, allowing 20 minutes for a good check at the end. However, remember that the questions are set at varying levels of difficulty, so these are only rough guides to help you pace yourself – in general, aim for at least 1 mark per minute. Show enough working so that you can still gain method marks even if the answer is wrong.

To ensure a reasonable coverage of the syllabus, some extended response questions may consist of unconnected parts, and will be clearly shown as such. Where a question has connected parts, make sure you use what you have worked out in the earlier parts to answer the later parts. Sometimes, too, you may find a clue in a later part which helps you to answer an earlier part. Generally, the extended response questions will start quite easily and will become relatively harder. It is crucial that you show full working and clear reasoning in these questions.

Each of papers 1 and 2 require full knowledge of the core syllabus and each is worth 30% of the final total.

Paper 3 (1 hour) is worth 20% and contains about 5 questions on your chosen option topic, all of which you must attempt to answer. These will be extended response questions and, where possible, they will begin with core topics which will then lead in to the option topic. Generally, 15 of the 60 marks will be allocated to core material. In the Discrete Mathematics option, there is little of the core material which is relevant, but the earlier parts of the questions will be of an equivalent level to the core.

▤ A reminder that you must *not* use calculator notation in exam questions. If you write normalcdf(100,120,116,8)=0.669 instead of showing appropriate working with mathematical notation, you could well lose marks – and if the answer is wrong you will gain no method marks. Similarly, if you calculate a definite integral on your GDC, make sure you write down the integral correctly as your working; calculator notation such as fnInt is unacceptable.

PRACTICE QUESTIONS

The questions which follow are not designed to cover every aspect of the syllabus, nor are they exam style questions. Their purpose is to give you some practice in the *basics*: if you cannot, for example, rearrange an equation with a log function in it, or correctly identify which integral technique to use, then you may be getting questions wrong simply because of a lack of basic techniques. You should answer all of these questions as part of your revision. If you get an answer wrong, find out why: then come back to it later, and see if you can get it right next time.

ALGEBRA

1. Find the 25th term and the sum of the first 54 terms of the sequence which begins: 3, 8, 13, 18 …
2. An arithmetic sequence has first term 7 and common difference 3.5. How many terms are required for the sum of the sequence to be 25830.
3. What is the 12th term and the sum to 18 terms of the sequence which begins 3, 12, 48, 192?
4. A geometric series has a first term 400, ten terms and a sum of 1295.67. What is the common ratio?
5. Why does the sum to infinity exist for the sequence 100, 80, 64, 51.2? Find S_{20} and S_∞ and also the percentage error in approximating S_∞ by S_{20}.
6. Write the recurring decimal 0.1343434….as a fraction in its simplest form.
7. Write $2 + 3\log_{10}x$ as a single logarithm.
8. Use logarithms to solve the equation $3.1^x = 10^{x-1}$. Answer to 4 decimal places.
9. If $s = 3 + 10e^{0.4t}$, use algebra to find t when $s = 23.54$
10. Solve the equation $4^x - 5 \times 2^x + 4 = 0$ *(Hint: Replace 2^x with y)*
11. Calculate $\log_3 30$.
12. A team of 3 is to be chosen from 9 volunteers for a general knowledge contest. How many possible teams are there? If the 9 volunteers consist of 5 boys and 4 girls, how many of the possible teams will have more girls than boys?
13. There are 26 letters in the alphabet and 10 numerical digits. A car has a registration number consisting of 3 letters followed by 2 digits. How many possibilities are there? And how many possibilities if all the letters must be different? If there is a free choice of letters, but the digits cannot begin with a 0, and must form an even number, how many possibilities are there?
14. Find the constant term in the expansion of $\left(3x - \dfrac{1}{x}\right)^6$.
15. Use mathematical induction to prove that the sum of the first n square numbers is given by the formula $S_n = \frac{1}{6}n(n+1)(2n+1)$.
16. Convert to modulus-argument form: $1 + i, 2 - 3i, -6i, (2 + i)^2$
17. Convert to Cartesian form: $[2, 60^\circ]$, $3(\cos\frac{5\pi}{3} + i\sin\frac{5\pi}{3})$, $4e^{i\pi}$
18. Solve $z^2 = 5 - 12i$.
19. Given that $2 + i$ is a root of the equation $z^3 - 11z + 20 - 0$, find the remaining roots.
20. Find the real number p for which $1 + pi$ is a solution of $z^2 - 2z + (p + 7) = 0$.
21. Find a cubic equation (with real coefficients) which has $3 + i$ and -2 as two of its roots.
22. Work out $(2 - i)^4$ using De Moivre's theorem. Give your answer in both modulus-argument and Cartesian forms. (The argument should be in radians).
23. Find the fifth roots of $1 + 2i$ using De Moivre's theorem.

FUNCTIONS AND EQUATIONS

1. Find the range of the function $f(x) = \dfrac{x^3 - 2}{x}$, $x < 0$.

2. Find the largest possible domain of the function $f : x \to \dfrac{1}{\sqrt{9 - 4x^2}}$

3. Why is the inverse of $f{:}x \to x(x - 2)$ not a function? Suggest a domain restriction which would ensure that $f^{-1}(x)$ *is* a function.

4. If $f{:}x \to x + 1$ and $g{:}x \to x^3$, find the function $(f \circ g)^{-1}$.

5. If $f{:}x \to (2x + 1)$ and $g{:}x \to \cos x$, $0 \le x \le \pi$, solve the equation $(g \circ f)(x) = 0.8$.

6. For the graph of $f(x) = \dfrac{e^{-x}}{(x + 1)^2}$, identify any horizontal and vertical asymptotes. Find the turning point, and the solutions of the equation $f(x) = 7$.

7. Define the transformations which will transform the graph of $y = \sqrt{x}$ into the graph of $y = 3\sqrt{a - x}$, where a is a constant. Sketch the two graphs on the same axes.

8. The graph of $f(x)$ has a horizontal asymptote at $y = -2$ and a vertical asymptote at $x = 1$. It passes through the origin. Sketch the graphs (all on separate axes) of $y = \dfrac{1}{f(x)}$, $y = f^{-1}(x)$, $y = |f(x)|$, $y = f(|x|)$.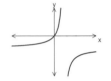

9. Use the quadratic formula to solve $x + 3 = \dfrac{2}{x}$.

10. Complete the square for: $x^2 - 4x + 2$, $2x^2 + 6x + 5$, $12 - 2x - x^2$.

11. For each of the quadratics in 10, write down the turning point and the line of symmetry.

12. Find the range of values of k for which $2x^2 + 2x + k = 0$ has two real, distinct solutions.

13. Use factorisation to find all the real solutions to $x^4 + 2x^2 - 15 = 0$.

14. Work out the inverses of these functions: $f(x) = 4 \times 3^x$; $f(x) = \dfrac{1}{\sqrt{\ln x + 4}}$; $f(x) = \dfrac{2x}{x - 1}$.

15. Solve the inequality $x^2 - 7x + 6 \le 0$. Hence solve $(e^x - 2)(e^x - 3) \le 2e^x$.

16. Solve the inequality $|4x - 1| < 5$

17. Find the values of x for which $|5 - 3x| \le |x + 1|$.

18. The graph of a cubic function cuts the x-axis at (-2, 0) and has a maximum at (4, 0). The y-intercept is at (0, -16). Write down its equation.

19. Prove that $(x + 2)$ is a factor of $x^4 - 3x^2 + 3x + 2$.

20. The polynomial $x^3 + ax^2 + bx + 5$ leaves a remainder of 2 when divided by $(x - 1)$ and a remainder of 9 when divided by $(x - 2)$. Find the values of a and b.

21. The graphs $y = x^3 - x^2 - x + 4$ and $y = x + 4$ intersect at A, B and C, where B is between A and C. Find the distance AC.

CIRCULAR FUNCTIONS AND TRIGONOMETRY

1. Convert to radians, giving answers in an exact form: 30°, 45°, 120°, 330°.

2. The sector of a circle with radius 5cm has an arc length of 12cm. Find the angle of the sector in radians, and its area.

3. Solve the equation $\sec^2\theta = 3$, $0^\circ \le \theta \le 360^\circ$.

4. If $\sin\theta = \frac{3}{8}$ and θ is obtuse, find the exact values of $\cos\theta$ and $\tan\theta$.

5. Using the data in question 4, work out the exact values of $\sin 2\theta$, $\cos 2\theta$ and $\tan 2\theta$.

6. Find an identity for $\sin 3\theta$ in terms of $\sin\theta$. (You will need to use the compound angle identities, the double angle identities and the Pythagorean identities).

7. Write down the domain and range of each of the functions $f(x) = \cos x$ and $f(x) = \cos^{-1}x$.

8. Write down the equation of the function shown right in the form $y = a\sin(b(x + c)) + d$
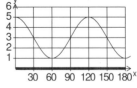

Use the trigonometric identities in questions 9 – 12.

9. Solve $2\sin x = 5\cos x$, $0 \le x \le 2\pi$

10. Solve $2\sin x = \cos 2x$, $-180^\circ \le x \le 180^\circ$

11. Solve $2\sin 2\theta = 3\sin\theta$, $0 \le \theta \le \pi$

12. Solve $3\sin x = \tan x$, $0 \leq x \leq 360^\circ$

13. Solve the following triangles (the triangle in each case is ABC):

   $BC = 6$cm, $C = 87^\circ$, $A = 45^\circ$. Find AB.

   $AB = 6$cm, $A = 87^\circ$, $AC = 5.4$cm. Find BC.

   $AB = 6$cm, $BC = 5.4$cm, $CA = 3.5$cm. Find B.

   $AB = BC = 5.2$cm. $B = 34^\circ$. Find AC.

   $AC = 6$cm, $C = 32^\circ$, $A = 90^\circ$. Find AB.

   $BC = 6$cm, $AB = 4$cm, $C = 25^\circ$. Find A. (Two possibilities).

14. Find the area of the first and second triangles in question 13.

15. Solve $\sin 2x = \sqrt{3} \cos x, 0 \leq x \leq \pi$, giving your answers in terms of π.

16. Express $\dfrac{\sqrt{3} + \tan x}{1 - \sqrt{3} \tan x}$ (x in radians) as a single trigonometric ratio.

17. The sides of a triangle are x, $x + 1$ and p, where $p > x + 1$. If the largest angle is 120°, find an expression for p in terms of x. Find x if $p = \sqrt{7}$.

MATRICES

1. If $A = \begin{pmatrix} 2 & 1 \\ 1 & -2 \end{pmatrix}$ and $B = \begin{pmatrix} 0 & 2 \\ -1 & 4 \end{pmatrix}$ find AB and prove that $\det A \times \det B = \det AB$.

2. Use a matrix method to solve $A\begin{pmatrix} x \\ y \end{pmatrix} = \begin{pmatrix} 3 \\ 5 \end{pmatrix}$, where A is as defined in question 1.

3. Find the integer p such that $\det \begin{pmatrix} 1 & p & 5 \\ -4 & 0 & 3 \\ p & 1 & -2 \end{pmatrix} = -27$.

4. If $P = \begin{pmatrix} 2 & 4 & 2 \\ -1 & 0 & 2 \\ 1 & 1 & 0 \end{pmatrix}$ and $Q = \begin{pmatrix} -2 & 2 & 8 \\ 2 & -2 & -6 \\ -1 & 2 & 4 \end{pmatrix}$ find PQ. Using the fact that for any matrix M, $MM^{-1} = I$, write down P^{-1}.

5. For what values of t does the matrix $S = \begin{pmatrix} t & -1 \\ -8 & 4t \end{pmatrix}$ not have an inverse?

6. If $t = 2$ in matrix S in question 5, find S^{-1}.

7. Given that $A = \begin{pmatrix} 3 & -2 \\ -3 & 4 \end{pmatrix}$ and $I = \begin{pmatrix} 1 & 0 \\ 0 & 1 \end{pmatrix}$, find the values of λ for which $A - \lambda I$ is a singular matrix.

8. Find the value of a for which the following system of equations does not have a unique solution:
$$\begin{cases} 4x - y + 2z = 1 \\ 2x + 3y = -6 \\ x - 2y + az = k \end{cases}$$

   How many solutions are there if $k = 3.5$, and how many if $k = 0$?

9. Solve the following system of equations:
$$\begin{cases} 3x - 2y + z = -4 \\ x + y - z = -2 \\ 2x + 3y = 4 \end{cases}$$

VECTORS

1. If A = (1, 4), B = (3, -2), C = (-1, -4) and D = (3, 5), find vectors **AB**, **BC**, **CD**, **AD**, **BD**. Which two vectors are parallel?
2. Find p and q such that $(pi + pj) + (3i + 2qj) = (qi + 18j)$.
3. If $r = 2i + 3j - \sqrt{3}k$, find the magnitude of r and the unit vector in the direction of r.
4. Find the value of a such that vectors $3i + 6k$ and $2i + j + ak$ are perpendicular.
5. If a, b and c are three non-zero vectors, which of the following statements must be true:
   (i) $a.b = a.c \Rightarrow b = c$ (ii) $a.b = 0 \Rightarrow a \perp b$ (iii) $a.(b + c) = a.b + a.c$ (iv) $a.(b.c) = (a.b).c$
6. Find the angle between the vectors $2i - 5j + k$ and $4i + 2j + 3k$.
7. A = (1, 2, 0), B = (1, 4, -3), C = (6, -2, 4), D = (0, 3, 3). Use scalar products to find the angle between lines AB and CD.
8. Write down the equation of the line AB (points as in number 7) in both vector and Cartesian form.
9. Find the point where the lines $i + j - k + \lambda(2i + j + 2k)$ and $\dfrac{x-2}{2} = \dfrac{9-y}{2} = \dfrac{z}{2}$ meet.
10. Prove that the lines $i + 2j + k + \lambda(-j + 4k)$ and $4k + \mu(-i + j - 5k)$ are skew.
11. How can you tell that two lines are parallel from their vector equations?
12. Find a vector which is perpendicular to both the lines in number 7.
13. If O is the origin, P = (1, 2, 1) and R = (-1, 4, 0), find point Q such that OPQR is a parallelogram. Use the cross product to find the area of the parallelogram.
14. Find the Cartesian equation of the plane which is parallel to the parallelogram in number 13, and which contains the point (3, 1, -2).
15. A = (1, 0, 1), B = (2, 2, 1), C = (3, -1, 0). Find the cross product **AB** × **AC** and hence the Cartesian equation of plane ABC.
16. Find where the line $4i + j + 2k + \lambda(-2i + j)$ meets the plane in question 15. Find also the angle between the line and the plane.
17. Find the point where the three planes $2x + 4y + z = 11$, $2x - y + 3z = 5$ and $x + z = 3$ intersect.
18. The plane $3x - 2y + 2z = 5$ contains the line $\dfrac{x-a}{2} = y - 1 = \dfrac{z+1}{b}$. Find the values of a and b.
19. A plane has vector equation $\begin{pmatrix} x \\ y \\ z \end{pmatrix} = \begin{pmatrix} 4 \\ -1 \\ 0 \end{pmatrix} + \lambda \begin{pmatrix} 1 \\ 1 \\ 2 \end{pmatrix} + \mu \begin{pmatrix} 0 \\ 2 \\ -1 \end{pmatrix}$. Find its Cartesian equation.

STATISTICS AND PROBABILITY

15.60	5.95	31.22	3.02	6.60	24.70	15.45	32.50	12.45	4.43
12.65	10.09	52.86	12.88	2.53	31.79	9.86	25.79	18.28	32.05
14.87	24.65	15.70	8.65	4.42	17.20	8.53	0.45	0.95	4.44
7.45	5.82	45.20	2.70	10.04	15.70	32.20	12.43	36.75	32.50
16.87	3.78	0.56	33.67	9.67	25.50	33.06	7.56	2.63	45.80

The amount spent (in €) by the first 50 people going into a shop is shown in the table above. Questions 1 to 9 refer to this table.

1. Is this data discrete or continuous?
2. Draw up a grouped frequency table (with first group €0.01 – €10.00). You should have 6 groups.
3. Which is the modal group?
4. Enter the mid-values of each group and the frequencies onto your GDC. Calculate estimates of the mean and the standard deviation. (Why "estimates")?
5. Draw a bar chart to represent the data.
6. Complete a cumulative frequency table for the data, and hence draw a cumulative frequency graph.
7. From the cumulative frequency graph, write down the median, the lower quartile, the upper quartile and calculate the interquartile range.
8. Draw a box and whisker plot for the data.

9. What was the least amount that the people in the top ten percentiles spent?
10. Two dice are thrown. What is P(at least one shows a number greater than 1)?
11. I have 6 red socks and 4 green socks in a draw. I take 2 out at random. Draw a tree diagram to show the possible outcomes and find P(the two socks do not match).
12. A and B are two events such that $P(A) = 0.2$, $P(B) = 0.5$ and $P(A \cup B) = 0.55$. Use a Venn Diagram to find: $P(A \cap B)$; $P(A' \cap B)$; $P(A|B)$; $P(B'|A)$.
13. Two dice are rolled. Find the probability that they show different numbers given that the total is 8.
14. Given that $P(A \cup B) = 0.7$, $P(A) = 0.6$ and that A and B are independent events, find $P(B)$.

15. Given that $P(A) = \frac{2}{3}$, $P(B|A) = \frac{2}{5}$ and $P(B|A') = \frac{1}{4}$, find $P(B')$ and $P(A' \cup B')$
16. The probability distribution for a discrete random variable X is as follows:

x	1	2	3	4	5
$P(X = x)$	0.3	0.35	k	$2k$	0.05

Find the value of k, the expected mean and the expected variance.
16. A probability density function which models the life expectancy of new-born infants is

given by: $f(x) = \begin{cases} kx^2(90 - x), & \text{for } 0 < x < 90 \\ 0 \text{ otherwise} \end{cases}$.

Find the value of k; the expected mean; the commonest age at which people would be expected to die; the median; and the proportion of the population who would be expected to live beyond 80.
17. For $X \sim B(12, 0.2)$, find $P(X = 3)$, $P(X \le 2)$, $P(X > 4)$. Find also the mean and the variance.
18. For $X \sim B(6, p)$, $P(X = 5) = 0.393216$. Find p.
19. For $X \sim B(4, 0.2)$, find $P(X = 3)$, without using your calculator *(Hint: you may find this easier if you work in fractions)*
20. For $X \sim P(3.2)$, find $P(X = 2)$, $P(X \le 4)$, $P(X \ge 5)$.
21. If $X \sim N(100, 5^2)$, find $P(X < 112)$, $P(X < 91)$, $P(95 < X < 101)$.
22. X is a Normally distributed variable with $\mu = 18$. If $P(X > 20) = 0.115965$, find the standard deviation.
23. For a certain type of potato, those with weight less than 100g are branded "small", and those with a weight over 125g are branded "large". In one batch, 2.55% of potatoes are small, 13.61% are large. Assuming the weights are Normally distributed, calculate the mean and standard deviation of the batch.

CALCULUS
1. Differentiate $f(x) = x^3$ and $f(x) = 2x^2 - 3x$ from first principles.
2. Differentiate these functions: (a) xe^{-x} (b) $3\sin^{-1}x$ (c) $\cos^2 2x$ (d) $4\sqrt{x} - 5$ (e) $2\ln(\cos x)$
(f) $\dfrac{x^2 - 2}{x}$ (g) $\dfrac{3x^3}{(x+1)}$ (h) $\sqrt{x^3 - 2}$ (i) $\sec^2 x$ (j) 3×4^x (k) $x^2 \log_3 x$ (l) $\dfrac{x^2}{\tan x}$ (m) $\ln(3 - x^2)$

3. If $y = \arccos(1 - 2x^2)$, find $\dfrac{dy}{dx}$, simplifying your answer.

4. Given that $y = \dfrac{x^2 - 1}{2x^2 + 1}$, find the set of values of x for which $\dfrac{dy}{dx} > 0$. Find the coordinates of any stationary points.

5. Find the equations of the tangent and normal to $y = 3\ln x$ at the point with x-coordinate 3.
6. Find the equations of the tangents to the curve $y^2 + 3xy + 4x^2 = 14$ at the points where $x = 1$.
7. Find the first and second derivatives of $y = xe^x$.
8. Find the coordinates of all stationary points and the point of inflexion on the graph of the function $f(x) = x^3 - 3x^2 + 1$. What is the gradient at the point of inflexion?

9. For the graph of the function $f(x) = \dfrac{x^2 - 1}{x}$ find: any axis intercepts; the vertical asymptote; the behaviour for large $|x|$; any turning points. Hence sketch the graph.

10. A circular oil slick is increasing in radius at the rate of 2m/min. Find the rate at which the area of the slick is increasing when its radius is 30m.

11. Integrate these functions: (a) $\int \sin 3x dx$ (b) $\int \dfrac{2}{x^2-1} dx$ (c) $\int \dfrac{1}{4+x^2} dx$ (d) $\int x\sqrt{2x-3} dx$

   (e) $\int \dfrac{1+x}{\sqrt{1-x^2}} dx$ (f) $\int 3\cos^2 x dx$ (g) $\int xe^{2x} dx$ (h) $\int \dfrac{1}{(2-x)^2} dx$ (i) $\int e^x \sin x dx$

12. Find the real number $k > 1$ for which $\int_1^k \left(1 + \dfrac{1}{x^2}\right) dx = \dfrac{3}{2}$

13. Find the area enclosed by the curve $y = 4x - x^2$ and the x-axis.
14. Find the area enclosed between the graph of $y = x\cos(x^2)$, the x-axis, $x = 0$ and the next positive x-intercept.
15. Find the area enclosed between the curves $y = 2x^2 + 3$ and $y = 10x - x^2$.
16. Find the volume enclosed when the area lying in the first quadrant and bounded by the curve $y = 2x^2 + 1$ between $y = 2$ and $y = 4$ is rotated 360º around the y-axis.
17. Find the solution of the differential equation $\dfrac{dy}{dx} = 2x(5 - x)$ given that $y = 3$ when $x = 0$.

18. Find the general solution of the differential equation $tx\dfrac{dx}{dt} = 1 + x^2$.

19. The displacement s of a particle from an origin O at time t seconds is $s = 2t^2 - 3t + 6$. Find the displacement, the velocity and the acceleration of the particle when $t = 1.5$.
20. A particle moves in a straight line. At time t secs its acceleration is given by $a = 3t - 1$. When $t = 0$, the velocity of the particle is 2 ms^{-1} and it is 3m from the origin. Find expressions for v and s in terms of t. Show that the particle is always moving away from the origin.
21. Differentiate $\dfrac{2 - 3x}{x^2 + 3x + 3}$ and hence find the turning points on the graph of $y = \dfrac{2 - 3x}{x^2 + 3x + 3}$
   Sketch the graph.

Answers to Practice Questions

ALGEBRA
1. 123, 7317 **2.** 120 **3.** 12582912, 6.87×10^{10} **4.** 0.7 **5.** $r = 0.8$, 494.24, 500, 1.15%
6. 133/990 **7.** $\log_{10} 100x^3$ **8.** 1.9660 **9.** 1.8 **10.** 0 or 2 **11.** 3.096 **12.** 84, 34
13. 1757600, 1560000, 7909200   **14.** −540
15. $\frac{1}{6} n(n+1)(2n+1) + (n+1)^2 = \frac{1}{6}(n+1)(n+2)(2n+3)$; $n = 1$ gives 1.

16. [$\sqrt{45}$, 45º], [$\sqrt{13}$, -56º], [6, -90º], [5, 53.1º] **17.** $1 + i\sqrt{3}$, $\frac{3}{2} - \frac{3\sqrt{3}}{2} i$, -4 **18.** $\pm(3 - 2i)$
19. 2 - i, -4 **20.** -2 **21.** $z^3 - 4z^2 - 2z + 20$ **22.** -7 −24i, [25, -1.855]
23. [1.17, (12.68 + 72n)º], $n = 1, 2, 3, 4$

FUNCTIONS AND EQUATIONS
1. $f(x) \geq 3$ **2.** $-1.5 \leq x \leq 1.5$ **3.** It's 1-many; $x \geq 1$ (others possible) **4.** $\sqrt[3]{(x - 1)}$ **5.** 2.32
6. $y = 0$, $x = -1$, (-3, 5.02), $x = -4.38$ or -0.512 or -2.06 **7.**

Reflect in y-axis, translate $\begin{pmatrix} a \\ 0 \end{pmatrix}$, stretch ×3 in y-direction.

8.

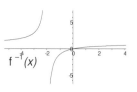
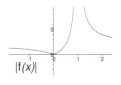
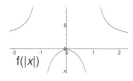

9. 0.562, -3.562 **10.** $(x-2)^2 - 2$, $2(x+1.5)^2 + 0.5$, $13 - (x+1)^2$ **11.** (2, -2), $x = 2$; (-1.5, 0.5),

$x = -1.5$; (-1, 13), $x = -1$ **12.** $k < 0.5$ **13.** $\pm\sqrt{3}$ **14.** $\log_3 \dfrac{x}{4}$, $e^{\left(\frac{1}{x^2}-4\right)}$, $\dfrac{x}{x-2}$ **15.** $1 < x < 6$, $0 < x < \ln 6$

16. $-1 < x < 1.5$ **17.** $1 \le x \le 3$ **18.** $y = 0.5(x+2)(x-4)^2$ **19.** $(-2)^4 - 3(-2)^2 + 3(-2) + 2 = 0$
20. $a = 2$, $b = -6$ **21.** $\sqrt{18}$

CIRCULAR FUNCTIONS AND TRIGONOMETRY

1. $\dfrac{\pi}{6}, \dfrac{\pi}{4}, \dfrac{\pi}{3}, \dfrac{11\pi}{6}$ **2.** 2.4, 30 **3.** 54.7º, 125.3º, 305.3º, 234.7º **4.** $-\dfrac{\sqrt{55}}{8}, -\dfrac{3}{\sqrt{55}}$

5. $\dfrac{3\sqrt{55}}{32}, \dfrac{23}{32}, \dfrac{3\sqrt{55}}{23}$ **6.** $3\sin\theta - 4\sin^3\theta$ **7.** All reals, $-1 \le \cos x \le 1$; $-1 \le x \le 1$, $0 \le \cos^{-1}x \le \pi$

8. $y = 2\sin(3(x+30)) + 3$ **9.** 1.19, 4.33 **10.** 21.5º, 158.5º **11.** 0, π, 0.723 **12.** 0º, 70.5º, 180º,
289.5º, 360º **13.** 8.47, 7.86, 35.3º, 3.04, 3.75, 39.3º or 140.7º **14.** 18.9, 16.2 **15.** 0, $\frac{\pi}{6}, \frac{5\pi}{6}$

16. $\tan(\frac{\pi}{3} + x)$ **17.** $p = \sqrt{3x^2 + 3x + 1}$, $x = 1$.

MATRICES

1. $\begin{pmatrix} -1 & 8 \\ 2 & -6 \end{pmatrix}$ **2.** $x = 2.2$, $y = -1.4$ **3.** 2 **4.** $\begin{pmatrix} 2 & 0 & 0 \\ 0 & 2 & 0 \\ 0 & 0 & 2 \end{pmatrix}$, $\begin{pmatrix} -1 & 1 & 4 \\ 1 & -1 & -3 \\ -0.5 & 1 & 2 \end{pmatrix}$ **5.** $\pm\sqrt{2}$ **6.** $\dfrac{1}{8}\begin{pmatrix} 8 & 1 \\ 8 & 2 \end{pmatrix}$

7. 1 or 6 **8.** 1, ∞, 0 **9.** $x = -1$, $y = 2$, $z = 3$

VECTORS

1. $\begin{pmatrix} 2 \\ -6 \end{pmatrix}, \begin{pmatrix} -4 \\ -2 \end{pmatrix}, \begin{pmatrix} 4 \\ 9 \end{pmatrix}, \begin{pmatrix} 2 \\ 1 \end{pmatrix}, \begin{pmatrix} 0 \\ 7 \end{pmatrix}$ BC, AD **2.** $p = 4$, $q = 7$ **3.** 4, $r = \frac{1}{2}i + \frac{3}{4}j - \frac{\sqrt{3}}{4}k$ **4.** -1 **5.** (ii), (iii)

6. 88.1º **7.** 62.7º **8.** $r = i + 2j + \lambda(2j - 3k)$, $x = 1, \dfrac{y-2}{2} = \dfrac{z}{-3}$ **9.** (7, 4, 5) **10.** To equate i and j,

$\mu = -1$, $\lambda = 3$. This gives $14k$ and $9k$, so do not intersect. Also not parallel, so skew.
11. Same direction vectors. **12.** $13i + 18j + 12k$ **13.** (0, 6, 1), $\sqrt{43}$ **14.** $4x + y - 6z = 25$
15. $2i - j + 5k = 7$ **16.** (0, 3, 2), 24.1º **17.** $\left(2\frac{2}{3}, 1\frac{1}{3}, \frac{1}{3}\right)$ **18.** 3, -2 **19.** $5x - y - 2z = 21$

STATISTICS AND PROBABILITY

1. Discrete. **2.**

0.01 – 10.00	10.01 – 20.00	20.01 – 30.00	30.01 – 40.00	40.01 – 50.00	50.01 – 60.00
20	14	5	8	2	1

3. 0.01 – 10.00 **4.** 17.2, 13.31; not using original data.
5.

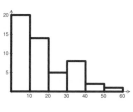

6.

€	≤10	≤ 20	≤ 30	≤ 40	≤ 50	≤60
c.f.	20	34	39	47	49	50

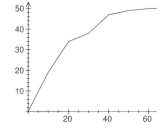

8.

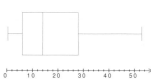

7. $Q_1 = 6$, $Q_2 = 14$, $Q_3 = 28$, IQR = 22

9. €38 **10.** 35/36 **11.** P(no match) = 24/45

12. 0.15, 0.35, 0.3, 0.25 **13.** 0.8

14. 0.25 **15.** $\frac{13}{20}, \frac{11}{15}$ **16.** 0.1, 2.35, 1.5275

17. 1.828×10^{-7}, 54, 60, 55.3, 6.3%

18. 0.236, 0.558, 0.0726; 2.4, 1.92

19. $\frac{256}{10000} = 0.0256$ **20.** 0.8

21. 0.209, 0.781, 0.219

22. 0.992, 0.0359, 0.421 **23.** 3.5 **24.** 116, 8.2

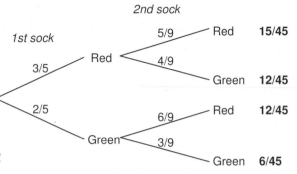

1st sock / 2nd sock

3/5 Red — 5/9 Red **15/45**, 4/9 Green **12/45**

2/5 Green — 6/9 Red **12/45**, 3/9 Green **6/45**

CALCULUS

1. $\text{Lim}_{x \to 0} \dfrac{(x+h)^3 - x^3}{h} = \text{Lim}_{x \to 0} \dfrac{3x^2 h + 3h^2 x + h^3}{h} = 3x^2$,

$\text{Lim}_{x \to 0} \dfrac{(2(x+h)^2 - 3(x+h)) - (2x^2 - 3x)}{h} = \text{Lim}_{x \to 0} \dfrac{4xh + 4h^2 - 3h}{h} = 4x - 3$ **2.** $e^{-x}(1 - x)$, $\dfrac{3}{\sqrt{1 - x^2}}$,

$-4\sin 2x \cos 2x$, $\dfrac{2}{\sqrt{x}}$, $-2\tan x$, $1 + \dfrac{2}{x^2}$, $\dfrac{3x^2(2x+3)}{(x+1)^2}$, $\dfrac{3x^2}{2\sqrt{x^3 - 2}}$, $2\sec^2 x \tan x$, $3\ln 4 \times 4^x$,

$\dfrac{x}{\ln 3} + 2x\log_3 x$, $\dfrac{2x \tan x - x^2 \sec^2 x}{\tan^2 x}$, $-\dfrac{2x}{3 - x^2}$ **3.** $\dfrac{2(1 - \cos x)}{\sqrt{2}\sin x}$ **4.** $x > 0$, (0, -1)

5. $y = x + 0.296$, $y = 6.296 - x$ **6.** $x + y + 4 = 0$, $y + 2x = 4$ **7.** $e^x(x + 1)$, $e^x(x + 2)$ **8.** (0, 1), (2, -3); (1, -1); -3 **9.** (-1, 0), (1, 0); $x = 0$; $f(x) \to x$; None.

10. 120π **11.** $-\frac{1}{3}\cos 3x + c$, $\ln\left|\dfrac{x-1}{x+1}\right| + c$, $2\tan^{-1}x + c$,

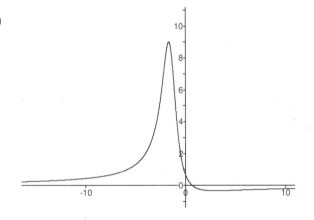

$\frac{1}{10}(2x-3)^{\frac{5}{2}} + \frac{1}{2}(2x-3)^{\frac{3}{2}} + c$, $\sin^{-1}x - \sqrt{(1 - x^2)} + c$, $\frac{3}{2}x + \frac{3}{4}\sin 2x + c$,

$\dfrac{x}{2}e^{2x} - \dfrac{1}{4}e^{2x} + c$, $\dfrac{1}{2 - x} + c$, $\frac{1}{2}e^x(\sin x - \cos x) + c$ **12.** 2 **13.** $10\frac{2}{3}$ **14.** 0.5 **15.** $9\frac{13}{27}$ **16.** 2π

17. $y = 5x^2 - \frac{2}{3}x^3 + 3$ **18.** $1 + x^2 = At^2$ **19.** 6, 3, 4 **20.** $v = 1.5t^2 - t + 2$, $s = 0.5t^3 - 0.5t^2 + 2t + 3$

$v \neq 0$ for any value of t (discriminant < 0). So v is always positive, and particle is moving away from the origin.

21. $\dfrac{3x^2 - 4x - 15}{(x^2 + 3x + 3)^2}$, $(3, -\frac{1}{3}), (-\frac{5}{3}, 9)$

Version 2.14